the Greater Evergreen Area guide

Including the communities:

Bailey, Conifer, Evergreen, Genesee, Indian Hills, Kittredge, Lookout Mountain, Morrison, and Pine

Kristen Raub Blum

Wanderlust Publishing
Seattle, Washington

On the cover: Ice skating on Evergreen Lake, Nicki Malenfant—Time Zone Photos. Mountain goats on Mt. Evans, Shirley Pasqua. Rock climbing on granite, Roger Whitehead. Evergreen 1925, Frank J. Duca (courtesy of Douglas Rouse).
On the back cover: Red Rocks Park, Lori Hladik. Wedding celebrations at Chief Hosa Lodge, © Wen Saunders, photojournalist (Boulder, CO 303-444-0064). Bears Inn Bed & Breakfast, courtesy of Darrell Jenkins.
Cover design: Dennis Blum, DB Designs
Editor: Tracy Wagers

Publisher's Cataloging-in-Publication
(Provided by Quality Books, Inc.)

Blum, Kristen Raub.
    The Greater Evergreen area guide : including the communities :
Bailey, Conifer, Evergreeen, Genesee, Indian Hills, Kittredge, Lookout
Mountain, Morrison, and Pine / Kristen Raub Blum. -- 1st ed.
    p. cm.
    Includes index.
    Preassigned LCCN: 98-96544
    ISBN: 0-9667085-0-4

    1. Evergreen (Colo.) Region--Guidebooks.
    2. Jefferson County (Colo.)--Guidebooks. I. Title.

F784.E9B58 1998   978.8'84
                             QB198-1467

ISBN: 0-9667085-0-4
Library of Congress Catalog Card Number: 98-96544

Attention: Quantity discounts are available on bulk purchases of this book to certain organizations and businesses. Please contact the publisher.

Wanderlust Publishing
P.O. Box 31515
Seattle, WA 98103-1515
1-888-879-9652
email: wanderlust@seanet.com

Acknowledgments

I would like to thank many people for believing in and helping to make this book possible. Many thanks to the Evergreen-Conifer Association of Realtors and other businesses who helped get this book into print. A special thanks to Maria Cook at the Evergreen-Conifer Association of Realtors who promoted this guide from the get-go and to Lincoln Gill who helped work out many of the details. Darrell Jenkins at Bears Inn supported this book from its inception and helped launch the book into print. Thanks also to my parents who have always encouraged me and provided support for this book's printing. I greatly appreciate everyone's faith in this entrepreneurial venture.

Compiling a book of this size takes a lot of cooperation. I especially would like to thank the photographers who donated their time and skill: Nicki Malenfant of Time Zone Photos, Frank and Shirley Pasqua, Doug Rouse, Lori Hladik, Roger Whitehead, Wen Saunders, and many businesses who donated photos or slides.

My editor, Tracy Wagers, played an integral part in this guide's professionalism, and I thank her for her fine tuning and friendship. Thanks also to Karen Hester at Dinosaur Ridge, John Steinle at the Hiwan Homestead Museum, and Roger Whitehead of Spirit, all of whom provided expertise in their fields and helped check the accuracy of various chapters.

The Greater Evergreen area community provided information and support at every turn, and interacting with the community was probably the best thing about writing this book. Thanks to Sue Wilson, Carolyn Campbell, and Linda Lovin for enthusiasm and advice.

Finally, thank you to my husband, Dennis, who put in his share of hours for this book, designed the cover and some of the graphics, and who always believes in me.

Table of Contents

Introduction
& How To Use this Book

The Greater Evergreen area, which adjoins the city of Denver, is a world away in many respects. Red rocks, clear mountain streams, wildflowers, and wildlife are the norm here. The area boasts two national forests, ten open space parks, a world-class fishing stream, several fourteeners, spectacular red rock monoliths, and numerous wilderness areas. Wildflowers burst into bloom everywhere in late spring and early summer, and aspens paint the mountains in golden glory every fall. It's not uncommon to see elk grazing on the side of the road and to catch a glimpse of a mountain lion or a bear.

Yet the breathtaking surroundings and the proximity to metropolitan Denver have also drawn an eclectic group of people to the area. Artists, writers, musicians, and actors make their home here, and even more talent comes to perform and play. Hence, you'll see top-notch theater productions, hear musicians from around the world, and can go gallery-hopping to your heart's content. There is something special for everyone here, and I hope that this book will help you find it.

Like any community, the greater Evergreen area faces many challenges as it grows. Places which once boasted small town atmosphere are on the verge of becoming bedroom communities, and people seem to always be leaving the place they call home. During the week, people commute to Denver, and on weekends, many commute to the ski resorts and the higher elevations for recreation. Traffic on the major highways sometimes becomes snarled, and for many, home becomes only a stopping place. The life of any community would feel this draining effect.

Luckily, the greater Evergreen area is full of life and strong citizens who support it and who are committed to preserving the quality of life. If you live here, join any of the organizations or attend community events, and you'll feel the lifeblood. If you're visiting, take some time to talk to the locals and get to know the character of the area.

But most importantly, stop and enjoy. I know that when I was living here, I often headed up to the higher mountains for my recreation, bypassing what was right outside my front door. It wasn't until researching this guide that I began to fully explore everything the area had to offer, and I could have kicked myself for not exploring it all earlier.

Go bouldering in Morrison. Visit the unique International Bell Museum. Take a backpacking trip into the Mt. Evans Wilderness. Treat yourself to a weekend at one of the amazing mountain inns. Celebrate your wedding or a special occasion at a historic lodge. Dine by candlelight overlooking the twinkling lights of Denver.

This book is for those of you fortunate to live here and for those of you coming to visit. Whereas Colorado guidebooks spend only several pages on the greater Evergreen area, this one covers it comprehensively. The near southwest mountains and their communities are included here: from Morrison up I-70 to Evergreen, across to Conifer, out to Pine and Bailey, back down Highway 285, and everything in between. See the map on the following page.

Unlike former books on the greater Evergreen area, this one covers all aspects of life: history, transportation, attractions, recreation, restaurants, lodging, celebrations, and practical information.

The structure is simple. Most of the nine chapters have their own introduction. Entries are then arranged alphabetically and begin with the important details you need to know: prices, addresses, directions, and phone numbers. Some of the chapters (Lodging, Restaurants, and Celebrations) include more detail. For example, in the Celebrations chapter, specific details on catering, the number of people the center holds, the time available, and other important information a bride might need to know are included first.

After this initial list of information, most entries then follow with a description. Use this description to help you choose which lodge fits your needs or which trail you have the energy to hike that day. Each review was done as candidly as possible, and no complimentary meals or accommodations were ever taken to influence the review.

Because the greater Evergreen area offers more opportunities than any book could contain, there are some omissions. Furthermore, information changes, sometimes surprisingly quickly. All of the details were checked as close to publication as possible. So always call ahead before you go. Remember that, depending on your location, some phone calls may be long distance.

I hope that this guide will give you the tools you need to begin your journey into one of the most exciting and inspiring areas in Colorado. While researching the book, I fell in love again with these mountain communities, and I hope you'll do the same. Remember, the words of the French poet Voltaire: "Cultiver votre jardin." Cultivate your garden. Everything you could ask for is in your own backyard.—Kristen Raub Blum

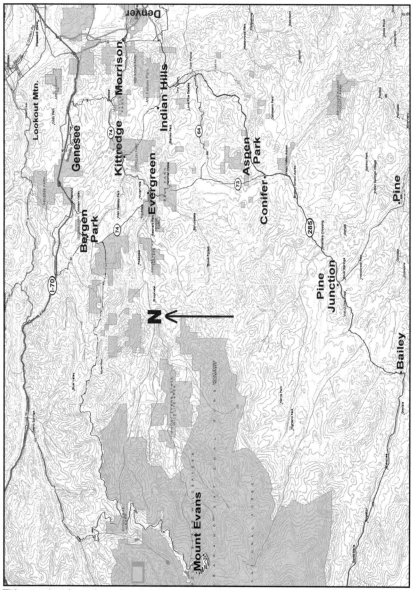

This map has been intentionally skewed to fit this page.   DB Designs

The greater Evergreen area—from Morrison to Mount Evans.

Chapter One
History

Although Colorado's geologic history stretches back billions of years, the story of the Front Range began close to 300 million years ago. It was then that tectonic uplifting formed the ancestral Rocky Mountains. Over the millions of years, these Ancestral Rockies eroded, and, in this region, all that remains of this ancient uplift are some formations at Red Rocks, the Flatirons, and stone structures at the Garden of the Gods.

From over 100 million to about 80 million years ago, the Great Cretaceous Seaway covered the central areas, north and south, of present-day North America. Ranging in width from 500 to 1200 miles across, this inland sea advanced and withdrew, depositing sediment and eventually leaving the area a lake-dotted plain. In this swampy lowland, dinosaurs flourished. Small therapods, such as Coleurosaurus and Iguanodons, roamed the land. Evidence of these creatures is visible today in the Dakota Hogback formation at Dinosaur Ridge. Seeing the rocks and dinosaur tracks, and walking the Hogback gives you a taste of this period in Colorado's geologic history.

Between 70 and 45 million years ago, the present ranges of the Rockies were created. Mount Evans' final stages were formed at this time. At Red Rocks, many rock formations exist from this time of the earth's development as well. What gave this area its high elevations was the movement of the entire Colorado Plateau which was raised as an irregular dome. Five-thousand-foot mountains became 10,000 feet high; 9,000-foot summits grew to 14,000-foot peaks, and the low plains leveled at about 6,000 feet.

Erosion, streams, rivers, and glaciers helped provide the finishing touches to the greater Evergreen area as we know it. Glaciers moved down the mountains and carved valleys. Water from the glaciers helped form streams, rivers like Bear Creek, and lakes like Summit Lake near Mount Evans.

K.Blum

The I-70 Geologic Cut is evidence of this region's rich geology.

THE PEOPLE CAME

In contrast to geologic history, human settlement in the area is recent. Native Americans were the first people to this area and used it as their hunting grounds and a summer campground. In the 1950s, a site near Morrison and the current Heritage Square was excavated, and Native American artifacts were found dating from 3000 to 1500 B.C. In 1996, the remains of a 3,000-year-old Native American woman were found in the Evergreen area.

Sioux, Ute, Arapaho, and Comanche tribes all traveled through this region, and their old trails became the first roads. Many buildings, roads, and towns honor the first Americans. Chief Hosa Lodge today is named for the famous Arapaho chief, and several place-names pay homage to Chief Colorow, a famous chief from the Ute tribe.

The first white settler in the region was Thomas Bergen, who arrived in 1859 and began homesteading the area now known as Bergen Park. He built a log cabin and then added on to it in the following years, building multiple cabins which served as his family's home, a hotel, a tavern, and oxen barns. Miners on their way to the gold fields stayed for 50 cents a night, a price which included a hot meal. Several toll roads were completed that ran through Bergen Park, and the area grew, reaching its peak population of 400 people in 1880. Bergen Park also served as the county seat of what was known as Ni-Wot County prior to 1861. However, when the railroad moved west, it bypassed Bergen Park, and the community lost its appeal and its people. By 1888, only 50 people remained.

Dr. Joseph Casto was another early settler. The town of Mount Vernon, situated where Matthews/Winters Park is today, was conceived in 1859 by Casto. Land was free to anyone who wanted to homestead. With its propitious location on the way to the gold fields, Mount Vernon was deemed a perfect location for a new city. Thirty-six-hundred small lots were mapped out, and families moved in, founding a school, church, stagecoach, and hotel building. The first governor of the Territory of Jefferson, Robert Steele, built his home there, and the town was on its way to becoming a prosperous community. However, with the advent of the Civil War, a corresponding decline in mining, and the growth of the nearby city of Golden, the town dissolved. By 1870, the town was virtually abandoned. Remnants of the old townsite, including a cemetery, can be found in Matthews/Winters Park today.

George Morrison was another important early settler. A Canadian stone mason who began life in the mountains in the town of Mount Vernon, Morrison moved to an area farther south, and in 1876, founded the town of Morrison. He built his family house, now the Cliff House Bed & Breakfast, as well as a school. Recognizing the importance of sandstone, gypsum, and limestone found in the area, he established quarries, a limestone plant, and a mill near Morrison. Some of this early sandstone can still be seen in the Brown Palace Hotel and in many historic Denver mansions. The town became known as the regional center for Denver's trade in lime.

To transport these materials to the city, George Morrison promoted the establishment of a branch of the Denver and South Park Railway in the area in 1874. The train transported materials from the town's businesses, as well as lumber, cattle, farm products, and tourists. Tourists rode the train from Denver for 60 cents round-trip, and many famous people traveled through the community in its early days. With the influx of activity, Morrison grew from a community of only 20 people in 1860 to one of 750 just 20 years later.

In part, tourists came to Morrison to see the inspirational Red Rocks Park, founded by John Brisben Walker. Walker, former owner of Cosmopolitan, purchased what was then known as the Garden of the Angels or Garden of the Titans and set about to preserve it for future generations. He was the first person to propose a system of mountain parks, a system which was adopted as an ordinance in 1912. Garden of the Angels officially opened on Memorial Day in 1906. In 1908, Walker built an incline railway up the face of Mount Morrison and added a dance pavilion to the park. On top of Mount Falcon, he built a $50,000 mansion (at 1908 prices) where his family lived for ten years before it was struck by lightning and burned. Walker had also proposed and laid the cornerstone for a summer home for the United States presidents, but he never followed through with his dreams because of financial failure. Remains of his mansion and the summer home for the presidents are still visible today on Mount Falcon.

Tourists also came by train to Morrison so that they could take the stagecoach on to Evergreen. Originally, Evergreen was called "The Post," after early settler Amos Post, Thomas Bergen's son-in-law. Another early settler, D.P. Wilmot, changed the town's name to Evergreen in 1875, inspired by the multitude of coniferous trees. In fact, Evergreen was known as the Blue Spruce Capital of the World because

Frank J. Duca
Courtesy of Douglas Rouse

Evergreen in the 1900s was known as a resort community.

the Colorado Blue Spruce was first discovered and named in Evergreen in 1862 by Dr. C. Perry, a 19th century botanist.

Lumbering and ranching were major Evergreen businesses in those days. Many Swedish immigrants migrated to Evergreen to work in the lumber mills. By 1895, there were seven saw mills in Evergreen, and piles of lumber lined Evergreen's main street, ready for hauling to Morrison and Denver. By the turn of the century, much of Evergreen was timbered out.

By 1900, Evergreen became known as a summer resort community. In summer, its population tripled, with visitors coming to enjoy the many resorts and relaxing mountain ambience. When improved roads came to the area and the mountain park system began, more and more people discovered Evergreen as a summer getaway.

By the same token, the Platte Canyon area, including Bailey and Shawnee, blossomed as a resort community at the turn of the century. The Denver, South Park and Pacific Railroad opened up the area to visitors. In addition, the railroad transported timber and ice from this area down to Denver. Timber seemed in inexhaustible supply and was also converted to charcoal for use in Denver ore smelters. Ice was cut from the Platte River in winter and transported to Denver by using hay as an insulator. At McGraw Memorial Park in Bailey, you can still see artifacts from that time, including the Maddox Ice Company boat that ran until 1937.

Conifer went through more name changes than any place around. It was named Conifer in 1900 after the area's thick conifer groves. However, before it was Conifer, it was named Bradford Junction, Hutchison, Hutchinson, and Junction City. Originally, the community was a quiet place where homesteaders farmed, operated stage stops, and ran sawmills for a living. One of Conifer's original homesteads is still there today in Aspen Park. Built in 1889, the yellow Meyer Ranch House, then the Midway House, operated as a hotel on the stage run to Fairplay.

Kittredge was primarily the work of one man, Charles Marble Kittredge, who first moved to Denver in hopes of achieving better health. He got involved with real estate, introducing the bungalow-style house to Denver. In 1920, he moved his family to a 160-acre ranch in an area then known as Martin Luther Ranch. Charles Kittredge then built water tanks, bridges, roads, a school, and post office. Once the main highway was paved in 1940, the town of Kittredge became a greater draw for residents and tourists alike.

The Genesee community did not come into existence until the 1970s. Yet, in the late 1920s and 30s, the area was known for its fur farming. After World War I, silver fox furs became popular, and the foothills' climate proved ideal for producing it. At one time, there were 20 fox farms in the area. One of the most successful sat on the present-day location of the Genesee town center. After fox went out of fashion, mink and chinchilla were raised. Eventually, foreign markets and cheap synthetic furs brought an end to this local industry.

One of the earliest ski areas was also in present-day Genesee. In 1917, a ski course and jump were built at Inspiration Point on Genesee Mountain. The National Ski Tournament took place there in 1921, and the ski area proved popular, existing until the 1950s.

Other ski areas opened in the 60s and 70s in the mountains just outside Denver. Squaw Pass ran for 14 years off the road to Mt. Evans before finances and dry winters forced it out of business. Today, this same area is a popular destination for cross-country skiers. Arapaho East was developed by the same operator as Arapaho Basin and ran from 1972-1978. The chair lift at this early ski area cost only 40 cents per ride. It wasn't necessary to purchase a full day's ticket.

Lookout Mountain is also a fairly new community even though attempts were made early on to make it a desirable place to live. Developer Rees C. Vidler, who owned 2,100 acres on Lookout Mountain, tried to establish Lookout Mountain as a community. To entice people to his planned community and to provide a route since there were no roads, he built a funicular, or open-air tramway, up the mountain in 1912. Vidler hoped that riders would be intrigued by the mountain scenery and would want to purchase lots. His office just happened to be located at the top of the funicular. However, at that time, not enough people wanted to live in such an inaccessible place, and Vidler forfeited his dreams.

Around the same time, George Olinger, a member of the mortuary and cemetery family, decided to develop the area now known as Indian Hills. In the 1860s, John D. Parmalee had homesteaded in the area and had called it Parmalee Gulch. But Olinger was the one who tried to expand it into a prosperous mountain community. He bought 2200 acres of land from original homestead families and began advertising a planned summer home community with small lots such as you might find in a city. Building lots were $100 and up for a pair, and with a cabin attached, the lot cost $1100. Olinger proposed a golf course with clubhouse which didn't materialize, nor did the buyers he had hoped for. To help market the new development, he decided to construct an authentic Indian pueblo called Na-Te-So. The pueblo complex was modeled after traditional pueblos and contained a museum of Indian artifacts, workshops where Indians performed their craft, and a place where the public could see traditional dances. Although the pueblo attracted visitors to the area, his development scheme fell prone to the Depression. The site of the old pueblo has since been restored and is a private residence today in Indian Hills.

AND PEOPLE CONTINUE TO COME

Ironically, today people are flocking to the greater Evergreen area without the incentives of Indian pueblos, funiculars, and ski areas. For the last 40 years, foothills residents have seen their small communities bursting with bulldozers. Maintaining a healthy level of growth has become a serious issue.

In 1949, maps were drawn in Evergreen for the first scheduled subdivision. Hiwan Ranch, once a 30,000-acre parcel, was subdivided into developments now known as Hiwan Hills, El Pinal, Hiwan Country Club, and the Ridge at Hiwan. Soon after these plans were drawn up, Evergreen's downtown was modernized, attracting more businesses. Developers became more serious about the foothills. On Lookout Mountain, land was also subdivided and water rights purchased.

By the 1960s, builders began to market their homes to Denver residents, and the population in the Evergreen area grew at a rate of 12.3%. In the 1970s, the new I-70 highway made access easy, and the communities became more like bedroom communities. Population doubled. Denver bid for the 1976 Winter Olympics, and Evergreen was to be the site of many of the events. Denver's Olympic bid was not accepted; however, growth continued. In the 1980s, more commercial development was proposed, and after waiting through Colorado's oil bust, development flourished in the 1990s.

Today, the greater Evergreen area is home to over 50,000 people and comprises several of the fastest growing counties in the state. Jefferson County's foothills population is expected to double in the next 20 years, and Park County's population is also increasing at a rapid rate. No longer, it seems, are people being coaxed to this area. They're choosing the lifestyle. Home prices have soared. Exits to Interstate Highway 70 and Highway 285 have been improved to hold increased traffic flow. New retail centers are popping up, and fast food franchises filling in.

Evergreen's downtown intersection should be improved within the next several years to ease traffic congestion. By 2002, Highway 285 will stretch four lanes wide to Conifer, and along with it will come services and businesses. Incorporation of Evergreen and Conifer continues to be a hot topic.

To find out more about the greater Evergreen area's history, stop by the Hiwan Homestead Museum, operated through a partnership between Jefferson County Open Space and the Jefferson County Historical Society. Their library is open to the public and contains a wealth of newspaper articles, books, and reference material on the area. Also see the bibliography for a listing of historical books.

Jefferson County has a map and brochure of its historical sites, and the town of Morrison offers a walking tour map that can be picked up at the Morrison Natural History Museum. Take time to explore the main streets of these communities, look at the photos in various museums throughout the area, and you'll get an idea of what the place once was.

K. Blum

Hiwan Homestead Museum is home to the Jefferson County Historical Society's extensive library.

Chapter Two
Getting Here

In the 1850s, the first roads were built into the mountains. They were wagon toll roads, built on the old Indian trails through the canyons, and they transported miners and their equipment to the gold fields of the Rockies. Some of the first settlers to this area dreamed not of gold, but of roads, and it was in these roads that they believed they would make their fortune. Dr. Joseph Casto, who arrived in the area in 1859 and settled the town of Mt. Vernon, was one of these first engineers. He built the rough road up the present-day Mt. Vernon canyon. Rains often washed out sections of this road, and it could take as long as four days to journey into Denver. John D. Parmalee, who settled in 1860 into the town now called Indian Hills, had a similar vision and built two main routes in the foothills. His main accomplishment was the toll road up Turkey Creek Canyon, now Highway 285. In its early days, the road was steep and treacherous, and it often took many days to go only five miles due to road conditions and people's fears of Indians or bandits. Parmalee Gulch Road, which still bears his name today, was John Parmalee's other venture.

"Cement Bill" Williams was yet another early road dreamer. He built the infamous Lariat Trail, which reaches from Golden over Lookout Mountain. From 1911 to 1914, Williams constructed an engineering feat up the mountain, a road rising 2,000 feet which includes 56 perfectly banked curves (seven of these are hairpin). His road became part of the Denver Mountain Parks' Circle Tour and quickly became a favorite drive for Denverites. In 1918, over 116,000 cars passed over the Lariat Trail, quickly making it congested. Additional parks and scenic spots were created to divert traffic from this popular route. In the 1950s, sports car races took place on the road, and fans lined the sides of the route to watch racers attempt to break speed records. Today the same large stone pillars in Golden still mark the entrance to the Lariat Trail Road.

With the construction of I-70 in the 1970s and Highway 285, travel to the communities is easy today if you have a car. And with the widening of Highway 285 south toward Conifer, travel will continue to get even easier. The commute to Denver is quicker than most people think, and it also takes a lot less time from here to get to the ski resorts in the higher mountains.

Check road conditions before you go—especially during the winter. For local road conditions, call **303-639-1111**. For state highways, call **303-639-1234**.

GETTING TO THE COMMUNITIES

BY CAR

Aspen Park, Bailey, Conifer, Indian Hills
The driving distances from Denver are approximate and follow.
Aspen Park: 31 miles
Bailey: 40 miles
Conifer: 33 miles
Indian Hills: 23 miles
   Take Highway 285. **Aspen Park** sits just off the highway, and although you won't see an exit, you'll recognize it by the large meadow on the south side and the big Coney Island hot dog on the north. **Conifer** is a bit farther down Highway 285. The Safeway Center and shops mark the community of Conifer. If you keep heading south, you'll pass through Pine Junction and then **Bailey**—all on the highway. To reach **Indian Hills**, take the Indian Hills/Parmalee Gulch Road exit from Highway 285.

Bergen Park, Evergreen, Genesee, Lookout Mountain, Morrison
The driving distances from Denver are approximate and follow.
Bergen Park: 22 miles
Evergreen: 28 miles
Genesee: 17.5 miles
Lookout Mountain: 15 miles
Morrison: 14 miles
   Take I-70. Exits for all the towns are well-marked. **Genesee** and **Lookout Mountain** are just off the highway. The Evergreen and Bergen Park exit is El Rancho/Evergreen Parkway. **Bergen Park** is the first community you'll reach once off the exit. Continue past the Wal-Mart and El Rancho, and you'll soon see a sign for Bergen Park. **Evergreen** is farther on Evergreen Parkway. To reach **Morrison**, from

the Morrison exit, follow Route 26 south to the town center.

Alternative routes:

Evergreen can also be accessed by road from Highway 285, going through the towns of Indian Hills or Conifer (although this route is much longer). A nice scenic route to Evergreen, if you want to avoid the I-70 traffic, is to take the road early settlers used through Bear Creek Canyon. This road, which begins in Morrison (see directions below), becomes Highway 74 and takes you through a narrow slice of canyon with red rocks, aspen trees, Bear Creek, and several mountain parks. It's a popular route with bikers as well, so drive with awareness.

Morrison can also be reached from C-470 or Highway 285. Look for the Morrison exits and follow the signs until you get to town.

Kittredge and Pine

Both communities are off the main interstates. The driving distances from Denver are approximate and follow.

Kittredge: 22 miles

Pine: 46 miles

For **Kittredge**, take I-70 to the Evergreen Parkway exit and then head through Evergreen on Highway 74 all the way to Kittredge. Or you can take the scenic and shorter road through Morrison. Take the Morrison exit and follow Morrison Road which becomes Highway 74 through the canyon. You can also take Highway 285 to the Indian Hills exit and take Parmalee Gulch Road all the way to its end. To reach **Pine**, take Highway 285 to Pine Junction. Turn left or south and go six miles on County Road 126 to Pine. Buffalo Creek is a bit farther down the same road.

BY BUS

RTD buses run to and from downtown Denver and the Denver Tech Center to the southeast during the morning and evening commute hours only. Below are the routes. Fares vary depending on location. Call for schedules and fares (303-299-6000).

Aspen Park, Bailey, Conifer, and Indian Hills

Route U picks up at the Park-n-Rides along Highway 285 and delivers to the Denver Tech Center and Greenwood Plaza. **Route C** picks up at similar locations to the U bus and runs to the Civic Center Station in downtown Denver.

Bergen Park, Evergreen, Genesee, Lookout Mountain, Morrison
   Route E runs from the Evergreen Park-n-Ride through Bergen Park and stops at several points along I-70 before making its way to the Civic Center. **Route Z** follows a similar route but makes more stops and begins at Aspen Park

BY PLANE

Denver International Airport, DIA as it is commonly called, is 30-45 miles from many mountain communities. However, there are a few transportation options to help make the ride smoother. There are door-to-door shuttle services and a bus. The shuttles can pick you up throughout the entire area. Prices vary depending on where you live, and you need to make reservations. For the bus, which goes directly to DIA, you'll need to drive to Lakewood. Call DIA for information about the airport and transportation options (303-342-2000).

A Premier Limousine Service
303-986-2887
   Provides limousine and town car door-to-door service for residents to DIA. If you have a family or group of people heading to the airport, the price is fairly reasonable.

American Transport
303-779-8289
   Provides town cars to DIA as well as downtown Denver and Colorado Springs at taxi cab prices. This service is also door-to-door.

SkyRide
303-299-6000
   Public bus service to DIA. The closest location to catch this bus is at the Cold Spring Park-n-Ride at the Federal Center on Union and 6th Avenue. **Route AF** leaves this location every day from 3:30 a.m. to 10:10 p.m. and returns to the location from DIA from 6:45 a.m. to 12:45 a.m. Allow about one hour and twenty minutes for the ride. The fare is approximately $8 one-way.

Superior Shuttle
303-399-2812
fax: 303-399-4355
email: adamti@aol.com
   Offers door-to-door service. This is a small family business that picks and drops off door-to-door, 24 hours a day, every day of the week.

GETTING AROUND

K. Blum

*By motorcycle is a popular way to get to and
around the foothills.*

Because the foothills' communities and attractions are so spread out, the best way to get around is by car. Buses do stop on their morning and evening routes around Evergreen, but they are geared toward commuters. Once in the communities, such as Evergreen or Morrison, walking is the best way to go. The towns are small enough and easy to get around. Many bikers love the canyon roads of the foothills, and by motorcycle is often a unique way to see the sites. Road bikes provide a nice non-motorized way to see the different towns; however, the roads are curvy, steep in spots, and usually there are a lot of cars. There is currently no taxi service in the area, although with the expected growth, things could change. Overall, drive with care in the mountains. Take it easy and watch for recreationalists, wildlife, and road hazards.

Chapter Three
Attractions

With several top tourist destinations in Colorado, museums that preserve mountain memories, dinosaur tracks, great theater, and some of the best places to see music and mingle, the mountain communities just outside Denver offer more attractions than you might think. Because of Denver's draw with its million-dollar sports complexes, nationally recognized theater, and rollercoasters, many don't look beyond the city. But the towns of Evergreen, Morrison, Conifer, and the surrounding communities offer top-notch arts, culture, and entertainment.

Dinosaurs first thought the area was a good tramping ground, and a tour along Dinosaur Ridge is just one of the exciting explorations in the foothills. At Buffalo Bill Memorial Museum and Grave, you'll step back into the Wild West, and at Hiwan Homestead Museum, you'll journey through the pioneer days and historical architecture from early Evergreen. At the International Bell Museum, the country's largest, you can see and hear ancient and new bells from around the world.

Interested visitors can pay homage to Saint Mother Cabrini at a place that seems like the top of the world just west of Morrison, and they can visit Tiny Town and see things as a kid again. Drive the highest paved road in the United States or indulge in one of the best day spas in the country.

You can join the crowd at Red Rocks amphitheater where giant uplifted rocks create acoustics known the world over or be among an eclectic gathering of people, from bikers to yuppies, at the infamous Little Bear bar where national and local bands play from the brassiere-lined stage.

Galleries, theaters, classes, and literature and poetry readings complete the picture of the entertainment life here. Before you think about delving into Denver's cultural scene and nightlife, try some of the greater Evergreen area's many attractions.

ANTIQUE STORES

Antique stores seem to be concentrated in Morrison, although there are a few scattered throughout the rest of the foothills. In Morrison, you can park and walk to the different shops which are all within several blocks of each other. Hours at some of the stores seem to be unpredictable, so if you're pressed for time, call before you go.

AUTOMOBILIA
103 1/2 Bear Creek Avenue
Morrison, CO
303-697-0750
Hours: Wednesday-Saturday: 10-6 p.m.; Sunday: 10-5 p.m.

With a unique offering of automobile memorabilia, this store is for the collector. Gas station collectibles, old gas pumps, pedal cars, toy cars, and automotive art work can all be found here. You'll recognize the shop by its vintage cars and car parts out front.

CHESHIRE CAT ANTIQUES & COLLECTIBLES
Corner of Highway 73/74 (Main Street)
Evergreen, CO
303-674-6053
Hours: 10 a.m.-5 p.m. (seven days/week)

This store has good antiques reminiscent of mountain décor—country furnishings, log furniture, and even a large stuffed bear. Their specialty is oak furniture and glassware, but they have a lot of everything.

COBWEB SHOPPE
28186 Highway 74 (Main Street)
Evergreen, CO
303-674-7833
Hours: Monday-Saturday: 10 a.m.-5 p.m.; Sunday: 11 a.m.-5 p.m.

In the heart of Evergreen, the Cobweb Shoppe buys and sell antiques and collectibles from fine china to jewelry and antiquarian books and gifts. There are some nice finds in this downtown Evergreen store.

EL MERCADO
120 Bear Creek Ave./Main Street
Morrison, CO
303-697-8361
Hours: normally 8 a.m.-5 p.m. (seven days/week) Call first.

One of Morrison's several antique stores, El Mercado, which is housed in an over 100-year old building, feels and smells like an antique store should. Amid the clutter inside and out, a variety of antique furnishings can be found.

K. Blum

El Mercado in Morrison looks and feels like an antique store.

LITTLE BITS OF YESTERDAY & TODAY
309 Bear Creek Avenue
Morrison, CO
303-697-8661
Hours: 11 a.m.-5:30 p.m. (seven days/week)

Another one of Morrison's antique haunts, this store specializes in Tiffany-style lamps but also has everything else you could want from books to bedpans. With a warm atmosphere, provided in part by the lighting of the Tiffany lamps, this place feels like an old home.

MORRISON ANTIQUES
307 Bear Creek Avenue
Morrison, CO
303-697-9545
Hours: Afternoons, Tuesday through Sunday

With one of the largest collections of printer's type and blocks, the kind that newspapers used to need before the advent of the computer, this store is worth checking out. The lady who runs it is a character, and there's plenty of "stuff" to find here.

OLD GLORY ANTIQUES
11825 Highway 285
Conifer, CO
303-838-4600
Hours: Monday-Saturday: 10 a.m.-5 p.m.; Sunday: 12-5 p.m.

Quality primitive antiques and folk art are the specialty here. The owner travels around the country looking for such unusual items. Every summer at Heritage Center in Lakewood, Old Glory sponsors a country fair with antique and folk art dealers from around the country.

REMEMBER WHEN ANTIQUES
26019 Highway 74
Kittredge, CO
303-674-7721
Hours: By appointment only

This store carries a good selection of primitives including quilts and original furniture. Call to inquire.

WESTERN TRAIL ANTIQUES & GIFTS
205 Bear Creek Avenue
Morrison, CO
303-697-9238
Hours: Saturday: 12 a.m.-5 p.m.; Thursday: 2-5 p.m. (call to arrange appointment all other hours)

With a yard and small house full of antiques, this store in Morrison offers plenty of opportunities for a find. The yard hosts outdoor antiques and farm implements, and inside, there's a special collection of copperware, teapots, knick-knacks, pots, and pans.

BOOKSTORES

CHESSLER BOOKS
29723 Troutdale Scenic Drive
Evergreen, CO
1-800-654-8502
303-670-0093
Hours: Monday-Saturday: 9 a.m.-5:30 p.m.

Specializing in mountaineering and climbing, Chessler Books is known throughout the United States as a great mail order company.

Yet, luckily for area residents, their home store is an adventurer's dream. Browse through stacks of recreation guides for places all over the world. They also have a good collection of nonfiction adventure literature, photography books, and maps. If you have any leaning toward world travel and adventure or are just longing to armchair travel, you'll love Chessler's.

CITY LIMITS
5510 Parmalee Gulch Road
Indian Hills, CO
303-697-3344
www.citylim.com
Hours: Tuesday-Friday: 10 a.m.-5 p.m.; Saturday: 9 a.m.-2 p.m.

Offering a selection of used and rare books and selective new titles, City Limits is both a cozy mountain bookstore and an extensive website for books. In Indian Hills, they're above the Indian Hills Espresso and are a friendly place where you can buy and sell used books. On the web, they're unique in that they have a research staff who will search for antiquarian books and out-of-print and hard-to-find titles and ship them to you anywhere in the world.

HAUNTED BOOKSHOP
Corner of Main Street and Highway 73
Evergreen, CO
303-670-4240
Hours: Monday-Saturday: 10 a.m.-7 p.m.; Sunday: noon-5 p.m.

Offering a general selection of used books, the Haunted Bookshop is another good book lover's find. Centrally located in downtown Evergreen, they're a good source for out-of-print and hard-to-find titles.

KR SYSTEMS, INC.
1 Delwood Drive #5
Bailey, CO
303-838-5509
Hours: Monday-Friday: 9 a.m.-6 p.m.; Saturday: 10 a.m.-4 p.m.; Sunday: Call first.

Since 1991, KR has brought quality outdoor recreation books, historical titles, nature, non-fiction, and western travel guides to the area. Their collection of rock and gem books is the best around, and they have a good selection of children's educational and nature books. In addition, KR is a United States Geological Survey dealer, so they carry a good selection of maps.

LOVIN'S BOOKS AND MUSIC

2982 Evergreen Parkway
Evergreen, CO
303-670-4549
Hours: Monday-Friday: 9 a.m.-6 p.m.; Saturday: 9 a.m.-5 p.m.
    Cozy and comfortable, with a café, many books, and a plethora of events, Lovin's is a great place to pass a day. During the summer, there are numerous events including readings and activities for children. Lovin's also hosts musical concerts, author readings, and book clubs throughout the year. Check out their newsletter for information.

MOUNTAIN BOOKS

25797 Conifer Road (Aspen Park Center)
Conifer, CO
303-838-4096
Hours: Monday-Friday: 9 a.m.-9 p.m.; Saturday-Sunday: 10 a.m.-5 p.m.
    This store offers a good selection of used and new books and is comfortable and friendly. Jesse McKean, who owns Mountain Books, is a good resource for the book lover.

CINEMA

BERGEN CINEMA

1204 Highway 74 (across from King Soopers)
Bergen Park, CO
303-670-5036
    First-run films on eight screens. Evening shows and matinees, weekends, summer, and school holidays. $6.50/adult; $5.50/student; $4.25/child.

DRIVES

    Although there are many spectacular drives in the foothills with views of the surrounding mountains and plains, there are two journeys that can't be missed. One is the trip up and over Guanella Pass, and the other is the drive to the top of Mt. Evans.

GUANELLA PASS SCENIC AND HISTORIC BYWAY

Directions: There are two ways to drive this route. You can take I-70 west from Denver to Georgetown. In Georgetown, follow the signs to Highway 62, Guanella Pass. Or, you can drive south on Highway 285 to

the town of Grant. From there, head north on Highway 62 to Guanella
Pass.

Phone: Clear Creek Ranger District (303-567-2901)

Guanella Pass Scenic and Historic Byway is a breathtaking drive.
Open year-round (as long as the road is plowed), this route can be
started either at Grant on the southern side or at Georgetown when
coming from the north. The road meanders through spruce forest,
mountain meadows, historic mining camps, and summits at 11,666
feet.

The drives around Mt. Evans are beautiful, especially during fall.

Douglas Rouse

Picnic and campgrounds line the route, and at every turn there's a
hiking or biking trail. To reach the historic townsites, you'll need a
high clearance vehicle, or you can bike or hike in. Historic Geneva
City can be reached by heading west from Guanella Pass at Duck
Creek Picnic Ground. Here, cabins and mills dot the hillsides. The
Waldorf Townsite, site of some of Colorado's early silver mines, can
be found by taking the Waldorf Cutoff, along the byway, south of
Georgetown.

At the summit of Guanella Pass, you'll find yourself in an alpine zone with a precious flowering plant and animal community. From here, you can take any number of trails or climb Mt. Bierstadt, one of the easiest fourteeners in Colorado. This area, although windy, is a great place to go snowshoeing as well.

In the fall, this drive is particularly scenic with the aspen trees aglow in golden colors. Call or stop by the Clear Creek Ranger Station in Idaho Springs (listed above) for more details on this drive.

MT. EVANS

Directions: There are also two ways to reach Mt. Evans. One way is to take I-70 west from Denver to the Evergreen exit and follow Evergreen Parkway three miles to Highway 103 where you'll turn right or west. There is a sign there for Mt. Evans and Squaw Pass. Follow Highway 103 until you reach Echo Lake where you'll see the road to Mt. Evans. Or, take I-70 west to Idaho Springs (second exit). Follow Highway 103 to Echo Lake and then take the road to the top. You'll pass the Clear Creek Ranger station and can pick up useful information here.

Cost: $6 per vehicle; pay just after Echo Lake on the road to the top; the pass is good for three days.

Phone: Clear Creek Ranger District (303-567-2901)

Because of its unsurpassed scenery, the drive to Mt. Evans is a popular route. Go when it's not peak tourist season but before the road closes. The road is generally closed after Labor Day through Memorial Day (depending on snow conditions). During summer, be prepared for a slow drive with many other vehicles. But with all this said, it's still absolutely worth the effort.

Built in 1915 as part of the Peak-to-Peak highway system, the road to Mt. Evans is the highest paved auto road in North America and a scenic byway. It provides the best 360-degree views anywhere around. At its top, at 14,130 feet, you can look down at Denver or out to snow-capped peaks. Mt. Evans is also considered a "living laboratory" where you can see one of Colorado's few virgin strands of bristlecone pines, some of which are 1600 years old. You'll cross three life zones including montane, subalpine forest, and alpine tundra on the way to the top.

In addition, the journey takes you on a wildlife safari with a very good chance to see bighorn sheep and mountain goats. Be warned, however, that these animals have been fed too much human food and are literally dying because of it. In the past year they have been killed crossing the road and have developed diseases. Take a memorable snapshot of these creatures, but don't feed them.

Also keep in mind the conditions at such a high elevation. It's often windy; storms come quickly, and the limited oxygen can be a shocker. There are hiking trails galore along the way, and this is a perfect place to take out-of-town visitors. You won't pay the fee until shortly past Echo Lake. Call or stop by the Clear Creek Ranger District in Idaho Springs (listed above) for more information.

EDUCATIONAL OPPORTUNITIES

The following centers have unique class offerings for adults. Many serve children as well. Many more classes for children can be found in the phone book or through the schools. Full addresses with zip code have been given so that you can write them for information.

ARTS ALIVE
P.O. Box 154
Conifer, CO 80433
303-763-6550
This non-profit organization provides arts and humanities educational programs to all ages. Some of their past classes have included a writer's workshop, T'ai Chi, and herb gardening. Call for information on their programs.

BODY MIND AWARENESS CENTER
29452 Dorothy Road
Evergreen, CO 80439
303-674-6047
Founded in a tranquil Evergreen location, this center specializes in superb hatha yoga classes for all levels, and holds dance, meditation, and various other personal growth workshops throughout the year. Call or write for more information and a brochure.

DOS MANOS WELLNESS CENTER
4600 Highway 73, suite AB/downtown Evergreen
Evergreen, CO 80437-0111
303-670-7300; 1-800-332-3969
As the name implies, this center provides the community with classes specializing in wellness and creativity. Native American beadwork, art therapy, meditation, color therapy, massage, and African drumming are just a few of the classes that have been offered at the center. In addition, Dos Manos has vocational education for health care professionals, holds celebrations and meetings, and offers massage and bodywork. Call or stop by for more information on their programs.

EVERGREEN POETS AND WRITERS
P.O. Box 7114
Evergreen, CO 80437
303-674-1330

A loosely formed organization of writers throughout the area, this organization has critique groups and open readings, runs the Evergreen Women's Press, and publishes *Buffalo Bones*, a poetry journal. Call for more information on their educational opportunities.

EVERGREEN PARK & RECREATION DISTRICT
P.O. Box 520
5300 S. Olive Road
Evergreen, CO 80437-0520
303-674-6441

Located behind Evergreen High School, the Evergreen Park and Recreation Center provides a recreational outlet and classes for the community (see Recreation chapter). But in addition, the center holds art classes for children and adults, leisure activities and classes for older adults (55 and over), and many other classes such as dog obedience, CPR, writing, and parenting.

RED ROCKS COMMUNITY COLLEGE MOUNTAIN CENTER
Conifer High School, 10441 Highway 73
Conifer, CO 80433
303-982-5233

Part of Jefferson County's community college, the Mountain Center offers a diverse range of classes for high school students and adults. Students may complete an Associate of Arts or Science degree at the Mountain Center, take teacher recertification classes, or upgrade business skills. Personal enrichment courses are also offered. To accommodate a variety of work schedules, classes run evenings, and there are also weekend-compressed courses, telecourses, and self-paced classes where students can learn at home. For Colorado residents, tuition is approximately $55 per credit hour. Non-resident tuition is approximately $253 per credit hour. There are senior discounts available for those age 60 and over. Call for a class schedule, and be sure to sign up early.

GALLERIES AND GIFT STORES

Many artists make their homes in the inspiring mountain communities, and hence, there are an unusually high number of galleries for a place of this size. Most of the galleries are clustered along Main Street Evergreen and in the Adobe Creek Arts Center in Kittredge. To reach the Adobe Creek Center, take Highway 74 to Kittredge. The center is on the south side of the street, across from the Tivoli Deer restaurant. Other interesting and fine art centers are scattered throughout the Evergreen area.

There are gift stores in the area carrying a range of collectibles. The historic Evergreen Hotel has been remodeled after a recent fire and now is home to quaint shops and galleries. Several gift stores are listed here, but for a complete listing, check out the phonebook or simply wander the streets of the various communities.

BEAR'S DEN
28055 Highway 74/Main Street (Evergreen Hotel Building)
Evergreen, CO
303-670-2327
Hours: 10 a.m.-5 p.m. (seven days/week)
For the bear lover and collector, this is your store. Collectible bears and bear accessories and the everyday bear can be found here.

BORN FREE GALLERY
1193 Bergen Parkway (King Soopers Plaza)
Evergreen, CO
303-670-2704
Hours: Monday-Friday: 10 a.m.-6 p.m.; Saturday: 10 a.m.-5 p.m.; Sunday: noon-5 p.m.; *Holidays* (November-December): 10 a.m.-7 p.m. (seven days/week)
Animals, animals, and more animals are the theme of this unique gallery in the Bergen Park Marketplace. Their pottery, painting, rugs, and collectibles come from artists all over the world.

DOS AMIGAS
28055 Main Street (Evergreen Hotel Building)
Evergreen, CO
303-674-1348
Hours: 10 a.m.-5:30 p.m. (seven days/week)
Mexican imports, gifts and home accessories are what makes this store special. Like the Bear's Den, it is located in the historic Evergreen Hotel Building, a unique place to visit on its own.

EVERGREEN ART COMPANY
3092 Evergreen Parkway
Evergreen, CO
303-670-1867; 1-800-452-9453

Purple Sage carries celestial items, herbs, herbal supplements, aromatherapy items, jewelry, and gifts leaning in that direction. Linda Stannard, certified acupuncturist, owns the store and does acupuncture next door. Call for more information.

SHADOW MOUNTAIN GALLERY

Adobe Creek Arts Center
26290 Highway 74
Kittredge, CO
303-670-3488
Hours: *Winter* Monday-Friday and Sunday: 11 a.m.-5 p.m.; Saturday: 10 a.m.-6 p.m.; *Summer* 10 a.m.-5 p.m. (seven days/week)

This co-op in the Adobe Creek Arts Center features Colorado artists and special exhibits. You can buy anything from gifts and tokens to fine art pieces worth thousands. Monday is senior discount day, and this co-op also has a special policy on fine wall pieces. You can take a piece home for 24 hours, try it out, and get a refund if you're not satisfied.

SILVER ARROW & SOUTHWEST ARTS

28159 Main Street
Evergreen, CO
303-670-0552
Hours: Monday-Saturday: 9:30 a.m.-5:30 p.m.; Sunday and holidays: 11 a.m.-5 p.m.

Authentic fine Native American jewelry along with southwestern art can be found at this Evergreen gallery. The art is reasonably priced and good for gifts or to wear yourself.

THE SOUTHWESTERN COLLECTION

6921 Highway 73
Evergreen, CO
303-670-3290
Hours: Monday-Saturday: 10:30 a.m.-5 p.m.

Another gallery focusing on Native American and southwestern art, this one feels authentic with Native American music playing in the background and a fine selection of pieces from Zapotec rugs to Navajo jewelry.

TA'TONKA

28045 Main Street
Evergreen, CO
303-670-9100

Hours: Tuesday-Saturday: 9:30 a.m.-5:30 p.m.; Sunday: 11 a.m.-4 p.m. (*Summer*—extended hours)

With a Native American, mountain-man bent, this store brings clothing, home furnishings, and the decorative arts to the mountain area. They have a good selection of custom leathers and wooden furniture. Ta'tonka Baby recently opened upstairs with a selection of unique baby clothing.

LIBRARIES

JEFFERSON COUNTY PUBLIC LIBRARY, Evergreen branch
5000 Highway 73
Evergreen, CO
303-674-0780
Hours: Monday-Thursday: 10 a.m.-9 p.m.; Friday-Saturday: 10 a.m.-5 p.m.; Sunday: noon-5 p.m.

Housed in a new building with a great back room to relax in and read near the fireplace, Evergreen's library is a pleasant place. In addition to its own collection and access to books throughout the metro area, the library has storytimes (toddler, pre-school, family night) and discovery days every other month where kids can explore different themes and participate in hands-on activities. They also offer Internet classes, library introductory tours, and classes on investment resources.

JEFFERSON COUNTY PUBLIC LIBRARY, Conifer branch
10441 Highway 73
Conifer, CO
303-982-5310
Hours: Monday-Thursday: 3-9 p.m.; Saturday: 10 a.m.-5 p.m.; Sunday: 12-5 p.m.

Conifer's library has 22,000 volumes, a good children's collection, and plenty of audiobooks for the commute. The library holds storytimes on Tuesday evenings, Explorer and Internet classes, and every month there are special programs. Located inside the Conifer high school, this library is in student use during the day but open to the public in the afternoon, evenings, and weekends.

JEFFERSON COUNTY HISTORICAL SOCIETY
4208 S. Timbervale Drive
Evergreen, CO
303-674-6262

Hours: Monday-Friday: 8 a.m.-5 p.m.

For the history buff, this library is a dream, with thousands of newspaper clippings, photos, and literature on foothills' history from its beginnings up to the present. The friendly staff there are available to help you research.

PARK COUNTY LIBRARY, Bailey branch
350 Bulldogger Road
Bailey, CO
303-838-5539
Hours: Monday, Tuesday, Thursday, Friday and Saturday: 9 a.m.-noon and 1-5 p.m.; Wednesday: 11:30 a.m.-7:30 p.m.

Providing a literary and research center for Park County, the Bailey branch is small but a good resource.

MUSEUMS

If you like hands-on museums with a specific focus, you'll enjoy the Greater Evergreen area's selection. These indoor and outdoor museums give you the opportunity to step back in time. Most of the museums focus on a famous person or epoch, rather than on general history.

BUFFALO BILL MEMORIAL MUSEUM AND GRAVE
987 1/2 Lookout Mountain Road
Golden, CO
303-526-0744
Hours: May 1-October 31: 9 a.m.-5 p.m. (seven days/week); *November 1-April 30* Tuesday-Sunday: 9 a.m.-4 p.m.
Cost: $3 adults; $1 children
Directions: Take I-70 west from Denver and get off at exit 256, Lookout Mountain. Follow the signs up Lookout Mountain Road to the museum.

One of the top five attractions in the Denver metro area, this museum is dedicated to the work of Buffalo Bill Cody: pony express rider, buffalo hunter, army scout, and showman. Visitors can tour the museum, view a film of his life, and revisit the Old West. Outside, Buffalo Bill's grave sits perched atop Lookout Mountain, a nice resting spot with views of the surrounding area. Special events take place at the museum throughout the year, including a re-enactment of Buffalo Bill's funeral.

Dinosaur tracks at Morrison's acclaimed Dinosaur Ridge.

Lori Hladik

DINOSAUR RIDGE
16831 W. Alameda Parkway
Morrison, CO
303-697-3466
www.dinoridge.org
Hours: Daylight
Cost: Free
Directions: Take I-70 west from Denver to the Morrison exit. Head south toward Morrison until you reach Dinosaur Ridge/Alameda Parkway. It comes off on your left, across from Red Rocks Park. The visitor center is across the ridge on the other side on Alameda Parkway.

It's hard to believe sometimes that 100 million years ago, Colorado was a flat lowland with freshwater streams, lakes, and roaming dinosaurs. But at Dinosaur Ridge, it seems easier to believe when you can see some of the over 300 dinosaur tracks and bones buried in the rock. In 1877, a local teacher discovered Jurassic dinosaur bones here which would bring the Morrison Hogback to fame. And now after a road has been dug through the area, more and more dinosaur remains are being unearthed. For kids, it's like seeing Jurassic Park live, and for adults, it's a potent reminder of the land before time. This is an outdoor museum where you can leisurely stroll the mile-long trail. On Dinosaur Discovery Days, which are monthly during the spring, summer, and fall, volunteers are stationed along the route to help interpret the findings. Otherwise, pick up a guided map at the visitor's center.

HIWAN HOMESTEAD MUSEUM
4208 S. Timbervale Drive
Evergreen, CO
303-674-6262

Hours: *September-May* Noon-5 p.m. (closed Monday); *June-August* 11 a.m.-5 p.m. (closed Monday)
Cost: Groups of 15 or more, $1/person
Directions: Take I-70 west from Denver to the Evergreen exit. Take Evergreen Parkway past Safeway. Look for a sign for Hiwan Homestead and follow this road uphill. Continue until you see Hiwan on your left.

Built in the early 1890s, this museum contains fine architecture and a sense of the early days of Evergreen. Dr. Josepha Douglas first owned the log structure and hired a well-known architect, Jock Spence, to convert it to a summer cottage. His signature work is evident in the octagonal rooms and stairstep designs found throughout the 17-room log cabin. Dr. Douglas, one of Colorado's first female doctors, owned the home with her husband, Canon Charles Winfred Douglas, an Episcopal priest. The chapel upstairs was the canon's personal chapel and today serves as a wedding chapel. The Buchanans were the last private owners of the home and changed the name to Hiwan, an Anglo-Saxon word meaning "members of a family household." The Buchanans raised prize Hereford cattle on their ranch. A good collection of Native American artifacts is found throughout the museum as well as relics of pioneer past. Personal tours are available and are free to small groups. During the school year, Hiwan runs educational programs for area fourth graders where the kids spend part of a day cooking, spinning, and experiencing changing hands-on exhibits.

INTERNATIONAL BELL MUSEUM
Upper Bear Creek Canyon
Evergreen, CO
303-674-3422
Hours: mid-May to mid-September: By appointment
Cost: $4 adults; $2 children
Directions: Take I-70 west to the Evergreen exit. Take Evergreen Parkway until you reach the lake. Turn right (west) on Upper Bear Creek Road and go approximately two miles. You'll see a sign on your right.

With a yard full of large bells, the outside of this museum introduces you to what's to come. Overall, this collection of more than 6,000 bells is the country's largest. Owner Winston Jones has been interested in bells since his first bicycle bell back in 1925. Since then he has amassed a collection of brass, glass, car, and altar bells, and even iron bells from coronations. There are bells from famous people like the "Unsinkable" Molly Brown, Queen Elizabeth, and Amelia Earhart. There are unique bells such as a Burmese temple gong from the 1700s, a bell from the first Cadillac, and goat bells found during an archaeological expedition in 250 B.C.

K. Blum

The country's largest selection of bells is found at the International Bell Museum in Evergreen.

Winston will personally take you through his museum, and he knows it all by heart. You'll learn the history behind the bells, some dating back to 1000 B.C., and Winston even rings some of the bells. All are in working condition. On July 4th every year, he rings the over 100 bells in his yard, and people come from all over to hear it. Take your time in this museum, and even if you've never thought much about bells, you'll come away with a deeper appreciation for them. Maybe it's their sound, combined with their visual impact, but the bells seem to bring history a little bit closer.

MORRISON NATURAL HISTORY MUSEUM
501 Highway 8
Morrison, CO
303-697-1873
Hours: Wednesday-Sunday: 1-4 p.m.
Cost: $1/person; $2.50/family; age five and under are free
Directions: Take C-470 to the Morrison exit. Head west through the town of Morrison until you reach the stoplight at Highway 8. Turn left (south) and go approximately one mile to the museum which is on your left.

If you're looking for a hands-on museum, this one is a good stop. You can learn about the history of the surrounding area and the plants and animals of the surrounding parks. The first Stegosaurus bones ever discovered were found at Dinosaur Ridge in Morrison, and some of these bones are now back at this history museum. Visitors can help remove some of the bones from the rock surrounding them. In addition, you get a chance to stain a fossil cast and hold or touch many of the live Colorado reptiles and amphibians on display here. Student groups even get the chance to participate in a fossil dig.

MUSIC

The following musical organizations are open to residents. They also perform concerts throughout the area during the year. Full addresses are listed so that you can write to them for more information.

EVERGREEN CHAMBER ORCHESTRA
P.O. Box 1371
Evergreen, CO 80437-1371
303-674-6707 or 303-674-7616
One of the better chamber orchestras in the metro area, this 45-member orchestra offers four concerts a year and a children's concert, in addition to several smaller recitals which take place in mountain area homes. For over 15 years, the chamber has included both mountain and Denver area residents, and they play a wide scope of music. Tickets for the performances are $10 for adults, with senior, student and children's prices available. Each fall there are tryouts for vacancies in the group. Dr. William Morse is the group's conductor.

EVERGREEN CHILDREN'S CHORALE
P.O. Box 3904
Evergreen, CO 80437-3904
303-674-9004
The chorale provides all children with the opportunity to perform musically. The Prelude chorale is open to second-fourth graders. The Chorale is geared toward fourth through eighth graders. There are concerts by these talented groups throughout the year, including a musical concert in December and a theatrical musical in June. *Cinderella*, and *Joseph and the Amazing Technicolor Dreamcoat* are some of the recent productions. Tickets run $10-12 for adults and $8-10 for students. They perform at Evergreen's Center Stage.

EVERGREEN CHORALE
P.O. Box 2103
Evergreen, CO 80437-2103
303-674-4002

With 90-plus members, this chorale performs two musical plays a year and two musical concerts, primarily at Center Stage in Evergreen. Since 1972, the chorale has been entertaining the Evergreen area. Productions such as *Godspell* and *Annie Get Your Gun* have been among some of the more recent productions, but the chorale performs everything from light opera to Broadway hits. Tickets run $12 for adults for the musical plays and $10 for the concerts. Call for a schedule or for tryouts.

MOUNTAIN COMMUNITY HANDBELL COALITION
P.O. Box 1238
Evergreen, CO 80437
303-674-2460 or 303-674-0378

This organization works to bring together the different handbell choirs throughout the area, and every other year, on the second Saturday in December, they sponsor the "bRing in the Holidays" handbell festival. With 15 handbell choirs, this festival (next one in 2000) is free and is held at various locations throughout the foothills. In addition, the coalition sponsors the Mountain Ringers, an auditioned handbell ensemble, which plays at different concerts throughout the area. All are free events. A seniors' outreach hand chime program is another group organized by the coalition. Call for more information.

NIGHTLIFE

The mountain areas offer several hot nightlife spots, and as the communities grow, there will probably be more opportunities for a night on the town. In the summertime, Red Rocks Amphitheater is every metro area resident's favorite concert venue (see Unique Sites). All year, check out these other listings.

BEAR CREEK TAVERN
25940 Highway 74
Kittredge, CO
303-674-9929
Hours: Monday-Thursday: 7 a.m.-9 p.m.; Friday: 7 a.m.-midnight; Saturday: 8 a.m.-midnight; Sunday: 8 a.m.-9 p.m.

Bear Creek Tavern has a jukebox, with a good variety of tunes, and pool tables, and is situated on the creek where you can watch the ducks and an occasional crane. They often have live music and serve food until 9 p.m. during the week and 10 p.m. on weekends.

THE LITTLE BEAR
28075 Main Street
Evergreen, CO
303-674-9991
Hours: Weekends: 11 a.m.-2 a.m.; weekdays: 11 a.m.-midnight

The Little Bear is the place for great concerts, pool, dancing, and people-watching. This local bar is popular with bikers, yuppies, and young and old alike. The old wooden building on Main Street is decorated inside with license plates, road signs from all over, and bras, which line the stage. National performers, including Willie Nelson, Fleetwood Mac, Leon Russell, and Neil McCoy have played here. Local performers take the stage here as well. Upstairs there are several pool tables, and downstairs, there is a dining area along with a small dance floor. For atmosphere and a good time, this place can't be missed.

Jim Krebs
Courtesy of the City and County of Denver

Red Rocks is every metro area resident's favorite concert venue.

SPAS

INDIAN SPRINGS RESORT
302 Soda Creek Road
Idaho Springs, CO
303-567-2191 or 303-623-2050
Hours: 7:30 a.m. to 10:30 a.m. (seven days/week)
Cost: Varies, depending on use. Call to inquire.
Directions: Take I-70 west from Denver to the first Idaho Springs exit. Go through town until you see the signs for Indian Springs Resort.

Although slightly west of the areas covered by this book, Indian Springs bears mentioning. First used by the Ute and Arapaho Indians, the springs have always been known for their healing powers. In 1866, Harrison Montague of Idaho Springs built a stone bath house and pool, and in 1869, he built the center part of what is now the Indian Springs Resort Hotel. In the early 1900s, the resort was enhanced with underground caves, a better swimming pool, and a more complete lodge. Frank and Jesse James, Sarah Bernhardt, and Walt Whitman are just a few notables who have experienced the springs' healing powers. Today the resort has 70 rooms, two single-sex geo-thermal caves, private indoor and outdoor baths, a mineral swimming pool, mud bath, massage services, and a restaurant and lounge. All water is natural hot mineral water. Prices are very reasonable (cheaper on weekdays) for the indulgence. Just off the highway on the way to the ski resorts, and 20 minutes from Evergreen, Indian Springs is accessible and good for relaxing sore stressed muscles. During the dry winters, the geo-thermal caves are a good weekly rehydrating routine.

TALL GRASS
997 Upper Bear Creek Road
Evergreen, CO
303-670-4444
Hours: Tuesday-Saturday: 9 a.m.-6 p.m.; Sunday: 12-6 p.m.
Cost: Depends on package
Directions: Take I-70 west to the Evergreen exit. Take Evergreen Parkway until you reach the lake. Turn right (west) on Upper Bear Creek Road and go 5.5 miles. Tall Grass will be on your right.

Located in a peaceful valley overlooking Mt. Evans, Tall Grass was rated one of the three best day spas in the country by *Travel and Leisure*. After a step inside this comfortable, quiet house, it's easy to see why. A stone fireplace with log-beamed ceilings and windows with views of the mountains immediately relax you. You can treat yourself to a facial, massage, body wrap, or a half- or full-day escape, which includes a facial, massage, nail services, and a refreshing spa lunch. In addition, the spa provides offers waxings and other services. Take time to linger and enjoy some pampering. Prices are similar to other spas of this caliber. Book your services at least a month in advance.

THEATER

Theater in the mountain communities, if you haven't seen it, is good, really good. It's a different experience than shelling out $20-65 dollars to see Broadway musicals and world-class plays in downtown Denver. Instead, you may pay close to $10 to see professionally done, well-known plays, in an intimate setting. The local theater scene up in the foothills draws from a wide pool of talented actors and is definitely something special. Center Stage, Evergreen's art venue located just east of downtown Evergreen on Iris Drive, hosts many of the mountain area productions. Evergreen South, located in Marshdale on Highway 74 near the intersection of Turkey Creek Road, is another temporary venue. Conifer's theater companies are in the process of building a community theater. Morrison Theatre, at 110 Stone Street in Morrison, is home to the Morrison Theatre Company. Full addresses are listed here to write for more information.

CONIFER MOUNTAIN THEATER COMPANY
11233 Conifer Mountain Road
Conifer, CO 80433
303-838-8196

A theater group for all ages, but with a focus on teens, the Conifer Mountain Theater Company puts on family-centered plays and comedies that help educate through entertainment. Along with the Conifer Stage Door Theater, this group wants to keep community theater alive in Conifer and presents plays around Conifer while they continue to search for a theater home.

CONIFER STAGE DOOR THEATRE
P.O. Box 71
Conifer, CO 80433
303-763-3050

With a troupe of players who deliver several main stage shows and a one-act festival each year, this theater fills another niche in the mountain community. At present, these professional productions are presented at venues around the Conifer community until the theater group finds a home. Usually, there's a Christmas presentation and summer performance of various comedies, dramas, and family shows. During the summer, this group also holds summer camps for kids. Tickets run $5-7.

EVERGREEN PLAYERS
P.O. Box 1271
Evergreen, CO 80439
303-674-4934

Established in the 1950s, this troupe is well-known throughout the area for their high-quality productions of drama, musicals, comedies, and experimental theater. This group, voted best in Jefferson County recently, presents four to six plays a year at Evergreen South and at Center Stage in Evergreen. Some of their recent productions have been *Dracula*, *A Tuna Christmas*, and *Working*, the musical. In addition, they hold workshops on acting, directing, and various aspects of theater throughout the year. Tickets to their professionally-done productions are $12 for adults and $10 for students and seniors.

Actor Gary Hathaway performs at the Morrison Theatre Company

Courtesy of Morrison Theatre Company

MORRISON THEATRE COMPANY
110 Stone Street
Morrison, CO 80465
303-697-0620

Up and running since 1990 in the historic town hall in Morrison, this company puts on four plays a year and offers children's acting workshops once a month. Each performance brings different actors from around the metro area for top-notch drama and comedies. The theater seats a cozy 80, and plays cost on average $10. Chris and Rick Bernstein have been running the theater since its inception and have a book out, titled *KIDZeye Theatre*, a collection of children's plays.

UNIQUE SITES

BOETTCHER MANSION
900 Colorow Road
Golden, CO
303-526-0855
Hours: Monday-Saturday: 8 a.m.-5 p.m. (except during event times); Evenings, holidays, Sundays by reservation
Cost: Free
Directions: Take I-70 west from Denver and get off at exit 256, Lookout Mountain. Follow the signs to Boettcher Mansion and the Lookout Mountain Nature Center.

Built by entrepreneur and philanthropist Charles Boettcher in 1917, this home stands as a testimony to history and an architectural movement. The Arts and Crafts Movement in architecture is represented in this historic mansion in its simplistic design and furnishings. At the turn of the century, this new movement rebelled against the ostentatious Victorian style and shoddy workmanship, and the Boettcher mansion, with its many natural materials, stenciling, and layout exemplifies it well. Outside, the grounds are alive with wildflowers, native plants, and ladybugs. Information on the unique architectural style and the history of the Boettcher family can be obtained at the mansion. A self-guided tour brochure is available. Next to the mansion is the new Lookout Mountain Nature Center and nature trail. On weekends the mansion is used for weddings and celebrations (see the Celebrations chapter).

EVERGREEN CEMETERY
Highway 74
Evergreen, CO
303-838-0443
Hours: Daylight
Cost: Free
Directions: Take I-70 west from Denver and get off at the Evergreen exit. Follow Evergreen Parkway past the Safeway. The cemetery is on your right, near Christ the King Church.

A unique short trip through Evergreen's past can be found in Evergreen's mountain cemetery. Overgrown with mountain vegetation, the cemetery has tombstones dating from the 1800s up to the present. Veterans, small children, mothers, fathers, and grandparents are buried here. Many of the individual plots are cared for with tombstones decorated with flowers, plus trinkets of sunglasses, fishing poles, Broncos paraphernalia, and photos. Some of the tombstones are no longer legible. It is one of the oldest cemeteries around.

HERITAGE SQUARE
18301 W. Colfax Avenue
Golden, CO
303-279-2789 or 303-277-0040
Hours: 10 a.m.-9 p.m. (seven days/week)
Cost: Admission to the grounds is free.
Directions: Take I-70 west from Denver and get off at the Morrison exit. Head north toward Golden two miles.

In the mid-50s, a large Disney-like amusement complex named "Magic Mountain" was planned for this site, but the dream did not materialize. Now, Heritage Square serves as a smaller version of this dream. Recreated to resemble an 1880s Victorian western town, Heritage Square is a good place to take out-of-town guests or the kids for a special day. There is a music hall, alpine slide, bungee jumping, children's rides, specialty shops, and restaurants.

I-70 GEOLOGIC CUT
Morrison, CO
Hours: Daylight
Cost: Free
Directions: Take I-70 west from Denver and get off at the Morrison exit. Turn north and look for the parking lot on your right (next to I-70).

An interesting slice of geologic history was uncovered when the road crew ran I-70 through the mountains. Representing more than 45 million years of geologic time, the rock that was deposited here is 140 to 95 millions years old. Along this short trail, there are interpretive signs which give you a brief geology lesson on the Rocky Mountains, and you can see the evidence in the multi-colored rock layers next to the trail. It's a good jumping-off point for adventures in the foothills.

MOTHER CABRINI SHRINE

20189 Cabrini Boulevard
Golden, CO
303-526-0758
Hours: *Summer* 7:30 a.m.-7:30 p.m (seven days/week); *Winter* 7 a.m.-5 p.m. (seven days/week); Gift shop open all year from 9 a.m.-5 p.m. (seven days/week)
Cost: Free (donation encouraged)
Directions: Take I-70 west from Denver to the Morrison exit. Turn north and take the frontage road, Highway 40, into the mountains. Follow the signs to the Mother Cabrini Shrine.

Look up in the sky as you head west on I-70 just after Morrison and you'll see a white alabaster Sacred Heart of Jesus overlooking Jefferson County. The statue, shrine, and chapel are open to visitors, and the site is spiritually invigorating. Founded by Mother Cabrini and originally used as a summer camp for orphans, the site became a shrine in 1946 when Mother Cabrini was canonized. Today, the shrine is a peaceful spot on an open landscape that looks over hills and the city below. It is quiet, with hawks often circling the top, beautifully landscaped grounds, and a spring where you can freshen water bottles after the hike to the statue. There are 373 steps up to the statue with stations of the cross along the way. Once at the top, the ten commandments encircle the 22-foot Sacred Heart statue as do white stones in the shape of a heart, arranged there by Mother Cabrini herself.

The Sacred Heart Statue at the Mother Cabrini Shrine watches over the Denver area.

K. Blum

MOUNT LINDO MEMORIAL PARK
5928 S. Turkey Creek Road
Morrison, CO
303-697-1227
Hours: 11 a.m.-4 p.m. (seven days/week)
Cost: Free
Directions: Take Highway 285 south from Denver to the South Turkey Creek Road exit, just past Indian Hills. Go about 0.25 miles (before Tiny Town). The cemetery road is on your left.

If you've been out at night in west Denver or headed into the mountains at night on Highway 285, you've seen the cross at Mount Lindo. An engineering marvel that won a world award, Mt. Lindo has been a cemetery since 1965 and remains a place of respect. Open to visitors, the drive up Mount Lindo is serene and affords pristine views of the surrounding country. With due respect, check out the cemetery on top of the mountain or look for the cross on a clear evening.

RED ROCKS PARK
12700 West Alameda Parkway
Morrison, CO
303-697-8935 (trading post)
303-697-8801 (concerts)
Hours: 5 a.m.-11 p.m. (seven days/week all year); Red Rocks Trading Post is open *Summer* Monday-Friday: 9 a.m.-7 p.m.; Saturday-Sunday: 9 a.m.-8 p.m. *Fall and Winter* 9 a.m.-6 p.m. (seven days/week)
Cost: Visiting the park is free. Concert tickets vary.
Directions: There are several ways to reach the park. Take I-70 west from Denver and get off at the Morrison exit. Head toward town, and you'll see an entrance to Red Rocks on your right (across from the Dinosaur Ridge Road). You can also get to Red Rocks from C-470. Take C-470 to the Morrison exit. Head through the town of Morrison and into the canyon. You'll see signs for Red Rocks on your right or north side of the road. Be aware that there also is a Red Rocks Elementary School.

Home to a world-renown amphitheater and some of the most spectacular geologic features around, Red Rocks is a place to visit both day and night. Formally opened in 1906 as the Garden of the Titans, Red Rocks initially became known as a concert venue only after the diligence of entrepreneur John Brisben Walker. Walker recognized the great natural acoustics of the theater and invited prima donna Mary Garden to sing there. In 1911, she sang "Ave Maria" and proclaimed that the theater would become world famous—and it has. George E. Cranmer, made the amphitheater into the spectacular venue it is today. Inspired by outdoor theaters in Greece and Italy, Cranmer wanted to work with the natural surroundings and hired an architect to complete the picture. The Civilian Conservation Corps built the amphitheater, and in 1941, Red Rocks was dedicated and has been home to concerts ever since. The Beatles, Jimi Hendrix, and Joan Baez are just of few of the hundreds of performers who have played at Red Rocks.

What makes the theater so unique are its natural acoustics. Try this out yourself when there's no concert. And the views! Situated between two 400-foot red sandstone formations, from the top seats you can see a panorama of Denver and the plains. When the moon rises over the plains and bursts into the sky in a brilliant red glow, it's something you'll never forget. But there's more. You can hike numerous trails throughout this 2700-acre park, picnic in the park, and spend time in the amphitheater when there's not a concert. Easter Sunrise Service, which has been a tradition since 1947, is another special event here.

TINY TOWN
6249 S. Turkey Creek Road
Tiny Town, CO
303-697-6829
Hours: *Memorial Day-Labor Day* 10 a.m.-5 p.m. (seven days/week)
May, September, and October 10 a.m.-5 p.m. (weekends)
Cost: $2.50 for adults; children $1.50; under age three are free. The train is an additional $1.
Directions: Take Highway 285 south from Denver to South Turkey Creek Road. Turn left or south and go 1/2 mile.

The oldest miniature town in the United States, Tiny Town has been open to the public since 1920. There are over 100 buildings, 20 of which are exact replicas of some of Colorado's historic buildings. A railroad powered by an authentic steam engine will take you around the town for a first glance. Then you're free to get out and explore; kids can even crawl inside some of the buildings. There's a replica of Denver Fire Station #1 from 1882, the Gates Rubber Company's first store in 1915, and a complete downtown with toy store, ice cream shop, movie theater, and grade school. Built in 1915 by George Turner for his daughter, the town quickly drew the attention of local residents and soon became a major tourist attraction. It's a good place to get a tiny look at history. The prices can't be beat.

Chapter Four
Recreation

The foothills are the gateway to the mountains and the ski slopes which beckon Denver area residents and tourists in the wintertime. But in itself, the greater Evergreen area offers a plethora of unique recreational opportunities. With 14,264 foot Mount Evans, the Morrison red rocks and hills, mountain lakes, streams, and national forest land, parks, and wilderness, this area hosts a variety of ecosystems and terrain. For the recreational enthusiast that means some of the best free spring skiing in the area, bike rides that challenge even the most advanced mountain and road bikers, and trails that meander from dense forests to alpine environments with stunning vistas stretching from the Continental Divide clear to the eastern plains of Colorado. Fishing, boating, hunting, horseback riding, climbing, and camping are all superb here. Even golfing is a special experience in this area with verdant hills and mountain scenery.

This chapter includes a selection of the greater Evergreen area's recreational opportunities with detailed descriptions and some trail maps. Although the subheadings divide recreation into individual activities, many of the trails' uses overlap. Trails are listed under the heading for the most popular activity. For example, the route to Bergen Peak in Elk Meadow Park is a favorite among serious mountain bikers, and so it is listed under the biking section. But for a longer day hike, the trip up Bergen Peak is wonderful. In the appendix you'll find all of the open space parks listed (even ones not included in this chapter), along with all of the opportunities each one offers. Use this if you want to pick an area to explore. Or browse through each subheading for your favorite activity and the most popular places to find it.

Remember, when headed into the mountains, play it safe. Weather in this region can change unpredictably, and lightning, hail, or whiteout blizzards can happen suddenly any time of year. In the summer, the earlier you get started in the day, the better, because of summer storms. Understand what you might encounter in the mountains. Hypothermia is one of the biggest killers of outdoor recreationalists. If going for extended times into the backcountry, read up or watch a video about this serious problem. Some of the first signs of hypothermia include shivering, slurred speech, mental confusion, and loss of coordination. Bring layers of clothing to help minimize this possibility. Altitude sickness should be a consideration, especially if you are not already acclimatized. A severe headache, shortness of breath, and sluggishness are common symptoms. Again read up about this potential dangerous sickness and descend if you're feeling sick on a hike! See the bibliography in the back of this guide for books on these topics.

To further insure an enjoyable day, read carefully about where you are going and abide by all regulations. Check with the organization or department which manages the area before you go, and read all posted signs. Check out the bibliograpy for other guides with recreational tips on the area. Try to live by the wilderness ethic to "Take only pictures and leave only footprints." With more and more use, areas tend to get run-down and less pristine, and conflicts sometimes develop between users. Be considerate when you explore so that we can all enjoy the mountains for years to come.

BIKING

On both road and trail in these mountain areas, the biker faces exciting challenges. With the hills and rocky terrain, many of the rides here are not for the beginner. For the novice mountain biker, some of the easy hiking trails in the open space parks also serve as bike trails and might be a better start. However, if you're adventurous and want to attempt some of these trails, you can try it! Just wear a helmet and be careful as you'll usually encounter quite a few switchbacks, steep inclines, quick descents, and some slippery, rocky turf.

Since mountain biking has become such a popular sport, there have been conflicts among trail users at the open space parks, and now at several of the parks certain trails are off-limits to mountain bikers. In parks where mountain biking is allowed, be considerate when whipping around sharp curves and follow the yield signs posted throughout all the parks. Make verbal contact with other trail users. In open space parks, equestrians and hikers always have the right of way. Also remember that riding, and even walking, on muddy trails speeds up erosion, and during the wet season, many trails may be closed.

Road bikers should only attempt the difficult routes if they're experienced as the roads are strenuous and steep, and often riders share the road with a lot of traffic. Off-tourist season is a better time to attemp-many of the roads, but even then, be prepared before you start one of the long routes. Many of the state's professional and Olympic bikers train on Squaw Pass. Many of the routes here marked "Novice" are paved trails and provide a good way to get light exercise. To get a feel for road biking on some of the area's steep mountain roads, try going out first with a guide such as **World Trek Expeditions** (303-202-1141 or 1-800-795-1142). They offer downhill trips. (You get a ride to the top.) One even starts at the top of Mt. Evans and drops 7,000 feet by the trip's end. Also, for both mountain bikers and road bikers, **Team Evergreen** (303-674-6048) is an Evergreen-based biking organization with good information and weekly rides.

Carry water on your rides in the mountains, along with rain gear, gloves, and sunscreen. Depending how far you are going, you might need to bring tools to fix your bike. Use the books listed in the bibliography to better acquaint you with the routes and also check with local shops for gear and more trail ideas. **Canyon Cycles** (26289 Highway 74, Kittredge, CO, 303-670-2728) and **Foothills Ski & Bike** (25948 Genesee Trail Road, Golden, CO, 303-526-2036) both sell and rent biking equipment. **Paragon Sports** (2962 Evergreen Parkway, Evergreen, CO, 303-670-0092) rents biking equipment, and all of these businesses know a lot about the area's routes.

All distances given are round-trip and approximate distances.

RATING:

Novice: A good route for any beginning biker or for those bikers more experienced wanting a short workout.

Moderately Easy: More challenging than the novice trails but within the grasp of most beginners.

Intermediate: Challenging rides for those with some experience.

Difficult: For the advanced rider. If you're not experienced, these trails are not recommended.

Biking the Colorado Trail on Kenosha Pass is one of many challenging bike rides in the area.

Lori Hladik

MOUNTAIN BIKING

BERGEN PEAK TRAIL

Distance: 10.3 miles
Rating: Difficult
Elevation gain: 1,980 feet
Location: Elk Meadow Park. From Denver, take I-70 west to the Evergreen exit. Follow Evergreen Parkway/Highway 74 to Stagecoach Boulevard in Evergreen (near Albertsons). Turn west and go 1.25 miles to the parking area.

Bergen Peak is one of the most technically difficult and exciting rides in Jefferson County. Begin on the Meadow View Trail from the parking lot and continue until the intersection for the Bergen Peak Trail. This first part of the trail (Meadow View) is fairly easy. Once on the Bergen Peak Trail, though, you'll continuously climb toward Bergen Peak at 9,708 feet. The trail passes through different ecosystems and travels over both smooth and rocky terrain and switchbacks. At the top, there are stunning vistas of five of Colorado's fourteeners and the plains. Take a breather and enjoy the views because the way down is fast and challenging. Take a left after coming off the Bergen Peak Trail and head down the Too Long Trail, named appropriately, through multiple steep switchbacks and back to the Meadow View Trail for a loop. Not for the faint of heart, this trail offers a chance for even advanced riders to test their endurance and maneuvering skills.

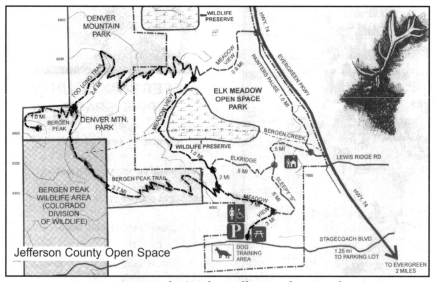

Bergen Peak Trail in Elk Meadow Park

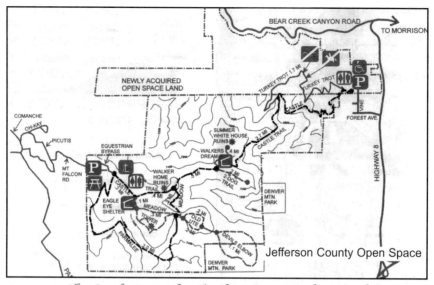

The Castle-Parmalee Trail in Mount Falcon Park

CASTLE-PARMALEE TRAIL

Distance: 9.4 miles
Rating: Difficult; Moderately Easy alternative
Elevation gain: 1700 feet
Location: Mount Falcon Park. Take C-470 to Highway 285. Head south on Highway 285 and take the Morrison exit. Follow Highway 8 toward town until you see signs for Mount Falcon.

Just one of the possibilities in Mount Falcon Park, this route is one of the most difficult, and one many locals love to do just after work. Begin climbing immediately from the parking lot up a series of switchbacks on the Castle Trail (the only trail open to mountain bikers on this side of the park). It's a tough climb but at the top, you are rewarded by views of the plains. You can return back to the parking lot here or continue on the Castle Trail. You'll see the ruins of an old home built by John Brisben Walker, a land speculator who owned Cosmopolitan magazine. Turn on the Meadow Trail and follow it until you get to the Parmalee Trail which takes you for a fun ride with challenging descents and climbs through the pines. Then you're back at the Castle Trail, near bathrooms and water. Take a right and head back down the Castle Trail to the parking lot. **Moderately Easy**: If you want an easier climb, begin your ride from the parking lot on the west side of the park with access from Parmalee Gulch Road in Indian Hills. From there you are already at the highest elevation in the park and can try any of the loop trails, including the Parmalee Trail.

COLORADO TRAIL

Distance: 12 miles
Rating: Intermediate
Elevation gain: 300 feet
Location: Kenosha Pass. Take Highway 285 to the summit of Kenosha Pass—approximately 60 miles from Denver. Park on the east side of the pass (you'll see many cars in the summer months).

This is just one of many rides on the Colorado Trail, which stretches 500 miles from Denver to Durango. You can also pick up the trail in the South Platte area near Pine, and there are a lot of opportunities for exploring. For this section of the trail, from the parking area head northwest of Highway 285 and follow the Colorado Trail signs through the campground. You'll climb through a wide aspen grove (great in the fall) and then encounter some sharp switchbacks. There's a difficult bridge across Guernsey Creek but then the trail levels out and continues on toward Jefferson Lake. Water is available at the Forest Service campgrounds in this area, and this is a good place to turn around if you're tired. If you want to continue, go west toward Georgia Pass. You'll cross over Jefferson Creek and manage some tough switchbacks. To the top of Georgia Pass, it's another six miles of rough and rocky riding, but there are amazing views from the top. Give yourself plenty of time for a breather and to enjoy the area before you head back to your car.

DAKOTA RIDGE

Distance: 7 miles
Rating: Difficult
Elevation gain: 970 feet
Location: Matthews/Winters Park. Take I-70 west and get off at the Morrison exit. Head south a short distance and park in the lot across from Matthews/Winters Park.

Considered another one of this county's challenging rides, Dakota Ridge, combined with the Matthews/Winters Park Trail, is a fun experience for the more advanced mountain biker. Begin climbing up the wide Dakota Ridge Trail on the east side of Highway 26 to the first summit where you'll be greeted by fantastic views of the surrounding area. This trail is fairly smooth and not too steep. Don't be fooled, though, as the trail suddenly turns into loose terrain with rocks, waterbars, and steps. You'll follow it down and then up to another summit where the trail finally becomes less rocky. Continue across and along Alameda Parkway until it meets up with the trail again on a southern bend in the road. From there, you proceed up to the final summit on the hogback. The descent down is quick and fun. You'll cross over Highway 26 and into Red Rocks Park. Pick up the Red Rocks Trail on

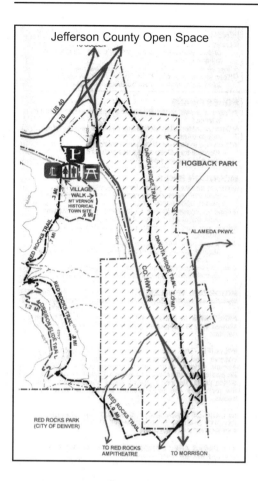

Jefferson County Open Space

HOGBACK PARK

ALAMEDA PKWY.

RED ROCKS PARK
(CITY OF DENVER)

TO RED ROCKS
AMPITHEATRE

TO MORRISON

*Dakota Ridge in Matthews/Winters
and the Hogback Park*

the right and head into Matthews Winters Park. This trail, which takes you back to where you started, is fairly smooth but involves some climbing. After you cross Cherry Gulch, the trail rolls downhill and is an easy ride. Overall, it's a good workout and could easily be done after a day on the job.

EVERGREEN MOUNTAIN LOOP TRAIL

Distance: 4.1 miles
Rating: Moderately Easy
Elevation gain: 500 feet
Location: Alderfer/Three Sisters Park. From Evergreen, take Highway 73 to Buffalo Park Road (at the Evergreen Library). Go 1.25 miles down Buffalo Park Road to the east entrance.

This trail is an advanced beginner's trail with enough incline to give you a fairly strenuous workout and a descent that will challenge your skills. What's nice about this trail is its wide, smooth terrain and its shade. It stays underneath the pine trees most of the way. Cross Buffalo Park Road and take the Evergreen Mountain Trail East. It climbs steadily up until it reaches the junction for the Summit Trail which leads to the top of Evergreen Mountain. If you want to take the Summit Trail, it will add about two miles and more than 300 feet to your trip. If not, continue on the Evergreen Mountain Trail which now heads west down a quick, steady descent. At the bottom, you'll meet up with the Ranch View Trail and return to the parking lot. (Map next page)

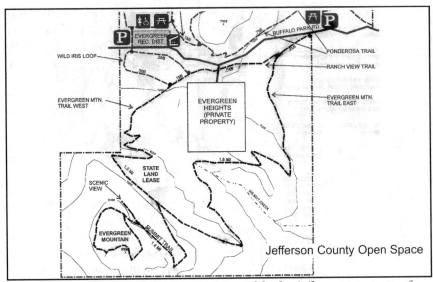

The Evergreen Mountain Loop in Alderfer/Three Sisters Park

MEADOW VIEW TRAIL
Distance: 5.5 miles
Rating: Moderately Easy
Elevation gain: 350 feet
Location: Elk Meadow Park. Same directions as the Bergen Peak Trail.

    Another trail in Elk Meadow Park, the Meadow View Trail is one of the best novice mountain biking trails in the Front Range. Undulating hills and a wide trail will turn even the most intrepid beginner into a fat tire fanatic. Begin on the Meadow View Trail and continue for 2.7 miles through forests and streams and a chance to see the Mt. Evans elk herd from fall through late spring. At Painters' Pause Trail, continue through the meadow to Sleepy "S" Trail and then back to the parking lot. There's enough up and down on this trail for the intermediate biker who wants a quick workout. This trail is popular and better on the weekdays.

ROAD BIKING

BEAR CREEK LAKE PARK
Distance: 10 miles round-trip
Rating: Novice
Elevation gain: Relatively level

Location: Morrison. Take Highway 285 to the Morrison exit and turn east to Bear Creek Lake Park. Park in the lot west of the gate, just off the highway.

With a wide concrete path, this bike route is a good one for the beginner or for the family. You'll wind through Bear Creek Lake Park, passing the swimming area and picnic tables en route. The trail is fairly level with only a slight climb at the Mt. Carbon Summit and Dam. The trail ends at the Fox Hollow Golf Course, and from there you can take Morrison Road back for a change of pace, but this road picks up some high-speed traffic. Otherwise, come back the same route and stop for a swim. You'll need to pay the daily admission fee of $3 per car. This path can also be combined with the following trail.

C-470 BIKE PATH

Distance: 4 miles each way
Rating: Novice
Elevation gain: Slight gain; rolling hills.
Location: Along the foothills. There are several access points for the ride, but the closest one is to take C-470 to the Morrison exit and head west about 1/8 mile to the parking lot at Morrison and Rooney Road.

This is also a great path for in-line skaters, a wide concrete way that takes you along the C-470 corridor. It's not the quietest bike route, but it's easy and accessible. From the parking area, head north on Rooney Road just up a slight hill to where you'll see the concrete path begin on your right. For a longer trip, combine this with the Bear Creek Lake Park route. To get a free map of this path and all other trails in the Denver metro area, call Colorado State Parks (303-866-3437).

MT. EVANS/SQUAW PASS

Distance: From Bergen Park, 32 miles; from Idaho Springs, 28 miles to the summit.
Rating: Difficult
Elevation gain: 7400 feet
Location: Arapaho National Forest. To reach the Bergen Park entrance, take Highway 73 to Squaw Pass Road and park in the lot connected to the park and baseball fields on the east side of the road.

One of the toughest rides around on the highest paved road in the United States, the trip up Squaw Pass to Mt. Evans is only for those in superb physical condition. Bring along extra gear as weather can change rapidly at such high altitudes. This description follows the route from the east side, from Bergen Park.

From the parking lot, take the Mt. Evans Road west. It steadily climbs through the forest and past housing subdivisions and is quite a challenge. Along the way you'll be rewarded with views of the Continental Divide. After 18 miles, you'll reach Echo Lake. Here there is shelter, a restaurant, gift shop, and plenty of places to picnic.

From Echo Lake, the road continues up to the summit for 14 miles and a whopping 3,661-foot elevation gain. This road is only open during the summer months and is often congested with traffic. In addition, watch out for mountain goats along the road which, because of tourists' feeding, have caused problems in recent years. After a short climb, you'll enter the alpine zone where trees, and consequently, shade, is scarce. Conditions get windy near the top, the views are amazing, and you can say you've biked a fourteener! The ride down is quick and often cold, but the hard work is done. If you feel adept at this ride, check out the Bob Cook Memorial Hill Climb.

The Bob Cook Memorial Hill Climb

Don't let "hill" in the name of this infamous bike race mislead you. The Bob Cook Memorial race climbs over 6,500 feet to its finish just below the Mt. Evans summit.

Since 1962, there has been a bike race on Mt. Evans, and in 1975, a man by the name of Bob Cook set a record time of two hours and three minutes for the course and held that record over the next several years. Cook joined the U.S. Olympic Cycling Team, but died of cancer in 1981, and this race has honored his name ever since.

Beginning in Idaho Springs, the race covers 28 miles to the summit. Every summer, serious cyclists set out to test their endurance on this tough ride, and times consistently remain under two hours.

MT. VERNON-EVERGREEN-MORRISON LOOP

Distance: 30.1 miles
Rating: Difficult; Intermediate alternative
Elevation gain: 1300 feet
Location: Morrison. Take I-70 to the Morrison exit. Park in the one of the lots at Matthews/Winters or in the lot across from Conoco on Highway 40.

A tough ride, this route will take you through several of this area's communities and provide you with spectacular views of the Continental Divide. The route begins where I-70 meets Highway 40 at Mt. Vernon Road, close to Matthews/Winters and the Hogback Park. Take Mt. Vernon Road or Highway 40, which parallels I-70, west for 5.5 miles until you reach the Park-n-Ride at Genesee and an on-ramp to I-70. Once a tollroad into the mountains, the Mt. Vernon Road is not too heavily traveled, but climbs steadily. At Mt. Vernon's junction with I-70, you have a spectacular view of the Great Divide and of the great buffalo which roam a fenced-in area just in front of you. Get on

I-70 (The highway has a wide shoulder.) for 1.5 miles until you reach the turn off for El Rancho or Evergreen Parkway. Be careful on I-70 and on Evergreen Parkway, which has recently turned into a speedy multi-lane road. To avoid some traffic, take a left at Bergen Park and follow Bergen Parkway until you meet up with Highway 74. Then take Highway 74 south toward Evergreen. Again, to avoid traffic, take a left at the road for the Hiwan Homestead Museum and follow this until its end. There's a park at the Hiwan Homestead Museum and several food options along the way, including a 7-11.

You will then be back on Highway 74, but past Main Street Evergreen and on a much smaller two-lane road with signs that alert vehicles to bikers. Follow this road through the canyon, passing Kittredge and Idledale and down to Morrison. You'll run beside the creek, and then it's a beautiful downhill ride into the town of Morrison. From Morrison, you're only three miles from your starting point. You could return right away by taking a left at the Dream Café back to Highway 26, or you could stop for a stroll around this historic town or for some tempting cheesecake at the Morrison Grocery. **Intermediate alternative**: On the Mt. Vernon Road take the turnoff for Lookout Mountain. To the top of Lookout Mountain it's four miles uphill, but the ride down is a gas. It's shorter and easier than doing the entire route described above.

BOATING

Despite the arid conditions of the foothills, there are several man-made lakes which offer boating activities during summer's warm days. For whitewater thrills, see the rafting section. **Evergreen Lake**, a favorite for winter sports, offers just as many summertime activities. The lake is located in the heart of Evergreen, just off Highway 74. **Soda Lakes** and **Bear Creek Lake** in Bear Creek Lake Park offer unique water activities along the Front Range. Soda Lakes and Bear Creek Lake are located just off Morrison Road and C-470. Anyone who drives C-470 regularly probably sees the water skiers on Little Soda Lake—very refreshing on a hot summer day. Bear Creek Lake provides the visitor with many recreational opportunities in addition to boating. You could spend a few days at the lake camping, fishing, swimming, and take advantage of the following boating activities. All the lakes allow private boats, but call for information. Fees are minimal and do change. Call for prices.

BOATING

BEAR CREEK LAKE (303-697-6159)
This lake, stocked with fish, is open just for fishermen and private boats, 10 horsepower or less. There is a minimal daily fee which includes your boat.

CANOEING

BIG SODA LAKE (303-697-6159)
Open only to non-motorized boats, Big Soda Lake rents canoes, and you also pay the daily park entrance fee.

EVERGREEN LAKE (303-674-0532; HOTLINE: 303-512-9300)
Canoes rent per hour with a deposit here. The lake is only open to non-motorized craft.

KAYAKING

BIG SODA LAKE (303-697-6159)
Sea kayaks rent here per hour. It's a good chance to practice some roll-over skills before heading out into the oceans of the world. Lessons are also available.

PADDLE BOATS

BIG SODA LAKE (303-697-6159)
Paddle boats rent per hour here. Similar prices to Evergreen Lake, but this might be more convenient for some Denver residents. Remember the daily entrance fee.

EVERGREEN LAKE (303-674-0532; HOTLINE: 303-512-9300)
Paddle boats make a fun trip with kids. They rent per 1/2 hour.

SAILING

BIG SODA LAKE (303-697-6159)
This lake also has sailboats for rent. Sunfish sailboats rent per hour from Memorial Day to Labor Day, and there is a daily pass fee. No certificate is required.

Evergreen Lake in the center of Evergreen is a popular summer recreation area.

Lori Hladik

EVERGREEN LAKE (303-674-0532; HOTLINE: 303-512-9300)

The sailing center is open seven days a week during summer months and several weekends in the spring and fall. Sailboats, small sunfish-type, may be rented for per hour with a deposit. Anyone renting a sailboat needs to be first certified by the lake sailing staff. Call to inquire. Private boats are allowed on the lake for a small fee during working hours with the same certification process listed above. In addition, Evergreen Lake offers sailing lessons for all ages, including a special senior class. Call 303-674-9463 to inquire.

WINDSURFING

BIG SODA LAKE (303-697-6159)

Sailboards are also rented by the hour at this lake during summer months with no certification. When the wind is right, windsurfing can be a lot of fun. Lessons are available as well. Call 303-426-6503 for lessons.

CAMPING

Camping is one of the most popular summertime activities for Colorado residents, and there are great campgrounds throughout this region, too many to name all below. In addition to established spots, this area has a number of backpacking options available in the **Arapaho National Forest** (303-567-2901), which begins at the edge of Evergreen, **Pike National Forest** (303-275-5610) to the southwest, and the **Mt. Evans State Wildlife Area** (303-291-7227). See the hiking section for extended trips which can take you into the backcountry for several days. It's definitely a worthwhile experience!

The first several sites mentioned under "Backcountry Sites" are established backcountry sites, usually with fire rings, grills, outhouses, and they might be just a short walk from the car. If there are trash cans, use them, but if not, pack out what you bring in. Avoid burning food or wrappings and leave the site in better condition than how you found it. Some of these sites accept reservations. If they do, this is marked in the introductory details. Call 1-800-280-CAMP and be prepared to give your reservation dates, camp name, type of camping equipment, and credit card number.

The sites under the subheading "Campgrounds" are good for a family excursion, for tourists visiting the area, or for hosting weekend guests. They are established sites, well-equipped with modern facilities, and are accessible to most types of vehicles.

BACKCOUNTRY SITES

CAMP ROCK CAMPGROUND
Location: Mt. Evans Elk Management Area, Mt. Evans Wilderness, a short walk from your car. You'll need a good high clearance vehicle, and the road back to the campground is only open from June 15 to Labor Day. Take Highway 74 in Evergreen to the north side of Evergreen Lake. Turn west on Upper Bear Creek Road; continue for 6.3 miles; take a right, which is really the continuation of Upper Bear Creek Road. Signs there point toward Singing River Ranch and Mt. Evans Outdoor Lab. Go for about two miles and stay to the right at the next Y intersection. At the second Y, take a left. Signs say State Wildlife Area and Mt. Evans Outdoor Lab. Go all the way to the main parking area; from there go right toward Camp Rock Campground (almost five miles). It's about a 45 minute beautiful drive from Evergreen.
Sites: 8
Reservations: No
Fee: None

The drive is long but well worth it as these campsites give you access to trails which lead into this wonderful slice of backcountry close to Evergreen. For more information on trails, see the hiking section. Call the Colorado Division of Wildlife (303-291-7227) for more information.

ECHO LAKE
Location: Mt. Evans. Take Highway 103 from either Bergen Park or Idaho Springs to Echo Lake. Campground is at the junction for the Mt. Evans Road.
Sites: 18

Reservations: Yes. 1-800-280-CAMP
Fee: $9.50

Close to the top of one of the state's fourteeners, Echo Lake campground is a good jumping off place for day hikes, the awesome drive to the top of Mt. Evans, and interesting wildlife watching. At 10,600 feet, this campground is nestled in the pines and is close to Echo Lake, the gift shop, and small café.

GENEVA PARK

Location: Guanella Pass. Take Highway 285 south to the town of Grant. Turn north along Forest Road 62, also known as the route to Guanella Pass. Geneva Park will be marked and on the west side of the highway.
Sites: 26
Reservations: No
Fee: $10

Geneva Park, in the Pike National Forest, is set in a nice quiet valley, close to good fishing, hiking and biking. Set-up your tent or small trailer here at 9800 feet and then take time to explore the miles of undisturbed wilderness around you. Because of its elevation, the camping season begins here around Memorial Day and extends into October. Fall is a particularly nice time here.

LONE ROCK CAMPGROUND

Location: South Platte. Take Highway 285 south toward Fairplay, and at Pine Junction, take County Road 126 past Buffalo Creek. Lone Rock Campground is close to Deckers, along the popular South Platte River route.
Sites: 20
Reservations: Yes. 1-800-280-CAMP
Fee: $10

This is just one of five campgrounds in this area of the South Platte River. Wigwam, Platte River, Ouzel, and Osprey are the other campgrounds, each with at least ten sites. Lone Rock is the biggest one, accommodating trailers under 16 feet. There is also a handicapped site and one with electricity. Water, tables, pit vault toilets, and fire grates are available here. If you're into fishing, this is the ideal place to spend the night and fish gold medal waters to your heart's content.

MAXWELL FALLS

Location: Brook Forest Road. To reach the sites, take Highway 73 to Brook Forest Road. Turn right or west and continue 6.5 miles past the Brook Forest Inn to an unmarked parking area and trailhead on the left.
Sites: 5-10

Camping at Maxwell Falls is a nice close-in wilderness experience.

K. Blum

Reservations: No
Fee: None
 These sites are just a short walk from the car. However, there is no central campground. Sites are dispersed along the creek, and it's a nice close-in area to spend the night and relax near the falls. However, this area tends to be heavily trafficked during early summer months and is in danger of being overused. Pack out what you bring in and be considerate of others and the nature around you. There are no restroom facilities as of this writing, so understand how to dispose of waste properly. When using these sites, stay at least 100 feet away from the water for all activities—cooking, cleaning, bathrooms, etc. Just off the parking area are a few sites. Others are located down the trail and on the right side of the creek.

WEST CHICAGO CREEK CAMPGROUND
Location: Mt. Evans. Take Highway 103 south from Idaho Springs toward Mt. Evans, about six miles to the turnoff for Forest Road 188. Go three miles on this road to the campground.
Sites: 16
Reservations: Yes. 1-800-280-CAMP
Fee: $8.50

Another campground close to Mt. Evans, West Chicago Creek is farther away from the tourist bustle than Echo Lake. These sites can accommodate vehicles up to 30 feet.

CAMPGROUNDS

CHIEF HOSA CAMPGROUND
Location: Chief Hosa, between Morrison and Evergreen. Take I-70 to the Chief Hosa exit. Campground is across from the lodge.
Phone: 303-526-7329
Sites: 200
Reservations: Yes
Fee: $13/vehicle. Full hook-ups and additional people are extra.

Close to I-70, this campground is under the evergreen trees, near hiking trails and buffalo herds, but it also has all the amenities. Two hundred sites sit on 55 acres, with water and electric hookups available. A heated swimming pool, laundry, and athletic area with outdoor games are all here. It's open mid-May to mid-September.

INDIAN PAINTBRUSH CAMPGROUND
Location: Bear Creek Lake Park. Take C-470 to Morrison Road and go east a short distance to Bear Creek Lake Park.
Phone: 303-697-6159
Sites: 52
Reservations: No
Fee: $7-10 with $3/vehicle entrance fee.

This campground gives campers access to all kinds of water activities, horseback riding, and a myriad of biking and hiking trails. It sits at the entrance to the foothills and is fairly exposed, but is also accessible and good for families. Open from April to October.

STAGE STOP CAMPGROUND
Location: Highway 285 between Indian Hills and Conifer. Take Highway 285 past Indian Hills to the sign for Stage Stop campground on the south side of the road.
Phone: 303-697-4901
Sites: 26
Reservations: Yes
Fee: $18 for two people. Additional charge for electrical hookups.

As the name implies, this is a good stopping grounds on the way toward Fairplay and the great west. It's about 30 minutes from Denver and has been locally operated for 32 years. Stage Stop is open mid-May to Labor Day.

CLIMBING

Since 1924, when climbing pioneer Robert Ellingwood made the first ascent of The Bishop in the South Platte area, the Greater Evergreen area has been known for its classic climbs. The Pike National Forest is home to some of the best granite climbing in all of Colorado. In addition, people from all over the world come to Morrison for its bouldering, and they come to the South Platte to attempt the Sphinx Crack, one of the most difficult crack climbs in the country. What also makes climbing in the region appealing is its proximity to Denver and the fact that most routes are accessible a good part of the year. Some of the routes are detailed here, but for more information on climbs, consult some of the books found in the bibliography. Clear Creek Canyon, just west of Golden, also offers some world-class sport climbing as does North Table Mountain, a great winter sport climbing spot.

Climbing is dangerous if you're a neophyte, and it's one of those activities where you'll need training or a guide. **Spirit** (303-697-9217), out of Indian Hills, teaches all levels of climbing and does guiding as well. Also check out the Denver rock climbing gyms, Recreational Equipment Inc. (REI), or the phone book for other classes and guiding services.

BOULDERING

MORRISON
Location: Take C-470 to the Morrison exit and go 0.5 miles toward town. You'll see parking spaces near the creek. Park here. The ridge is just opposite on the northeast side. There are many dirt trails which will take you from the road to the ridge and the boulders.

With names like "Hairy Scary Wall," "Sailor's Delight," and "Hogback Mama," the bouldering wall in Morrison runs the gamut of grades and offers fantastic bouldering. Because of its smooth south-facing rock, climbers will find this a good year-round spot. There are more than 65 bouldering routes with a lot of overhangs and top-rope problems which provide excitement for all levels of ability

CLIMBING

LOVER'S LEAP

Location: Three miles south of C-470 on Highway 285. You'll need to pass the giant rock on the south side of the highway, find a turnaround (the Indian Hills exit is probably the safest) and come back toward Denver. There is a parking pull-off area there, and you'll see trails scrambling down from there and across the creek. It's a bit of a hike in.

A 450-foot buttress in Turkey Creek Canyon, Lover's Leap is a good climbing crag close to Denver. Although several climbs, ranging from 5.6 to 5.12C in difficulty, exist here, the Lover's Leap route is the most popular at 5.7. A 5 pitch climb, this is a good experienced beginner's choice.

THE SPHINX CRACK

Location: Take Highway 285 to Pine Junction and then head south on County Road 126 to Pine. At Pine, take a left or east at the old gas station, and take the road which leads toward Sphinx Park. Go 0.25 miles and look for the large buttress on the right. There is a pull-off on the side of the road.

This climb in the South Platte area is one of the country's hardest crack climbs and to date has only seen a handful of ascents. People come from all over the world to attempt this crack. Ninety feet tall, the crack goes through the buttress of this large rock formation. There are almost no footholds, and it's a more-than-vertical climb with an overhanging wall. It's rated as a 5.13B climb, but most people rate it as 13C. This climb is obviously only for the advanced climber, and even then it's an extreme challenge.

Alpine Rescue Team

Formed in 1959, this all-volunteer, non-profit, search and rescue team is based out of Evergreen. It provides free assistance for lost travelers, injured climbers, and victims of river accidents and downed aircraft. Overall they are a life-saving force for all outdoor recreationalists.

Most of the team's missions are in Jefferson and Clear Creek Counties, but they also respond to calls throughout the state of Colorado and beyond.

In addition, the team educates the public about mountain safety. Their annual Avalanche Awareness Week offers outdoor enthusiasts a chance to learn about this danger in the backcountry.

Anyone who wishes to join the team or support them can contact them: Alpine Rescue Team, P.O. Box 934, Evergreen, Colorado 80439; 303-526-2417. If you have information about any backcountry accident, call 911 first.

FISHING

One of the most productive trout streams in the nation is the South Platte River, and there are numerous other fish-filled lakes and rivers in this region as well. Rainbow Trout, Wild Brown Trout, Tiger Muskies, and Cutthroat Trout, the state fish, swim the lakes and rivers of the area.

A fishing license is required for anyone 16 years and older in the state of Colorado. A 25-cent fee tacked onto the fishing license helps pay for search and rescue for any license holder and is a good idea for anyone exploring the backcountry. Short-term licenses can also be purchased, including a one-day license and a five-day license. Call the **Colorado Division of Wildlife** (303-297-1192) for more information. They also produce brochures on the state's gold medal waters and fishing hot spots.

In Evergreen, the acclaimed **Blue Quill Angler** (303-674-4700) is a complete fly-fishing shop and one of the only fully Orvis-endorsed schools and outfitters in the country. They offer fly-fishing classes and guiding trips into the South Platte. Check them out for gear and information.

BEAR CREEK
Location: Mt. Evans east through the Denver metro area. Access it along Highway 74 which runs from Morrison to Evergreen.

Bear Creek has stocked Rainbow, Wild Brown, Cutthroat, and Brook Trout. If you find the right spot, this river produces some good catches. Watch for private land as many parts of this creek are adjacent to private residences.

BEAR CREEK LAKE
Location: Bear Creek Lake Park. Take C-470 to the Morrison exit and head east. Bear Creek Lake Park is on the south side of Morrison road.

This large lake in Bear Creek Lake Park is stocked with Rainbow Trout, Smallmouth Bass, and Tiger Muskie. This is the only lake in the area where motorboats are allowed, 10 horsepower or less, and it's a good place for families.

BEARTRACK LAKES
Location: Mt. Evans Wilderness. Take Highway 74 in Evergreen to the north side of Evergreen Lake. Turn west on Upper Bear Creek Road; continue for 6.3 miles; take a right on the continuation of Upper Bear Creek Road. Signs there point toward Singing River Ranch and Mt. Evans Outdoor Lab. Go for two miles and stay to the right at the next Y

intersection. At the second Y, take a left. Signs say State Wildlife Area and Mt. Evans Outdoor Lab. Go all the way to the main parking area; from there, go right toward Camp Rock Campground (almost five miles). It's about a 1/2 hour beautiful drive from Evergreen.

Beartrack Lakes are a good day's hike up into the Mt. Evans Wilderness and popular with fishermen during summer weekends. The lake is situated in a bowl at the base of several peaks and a beautiful spot, but won't provide solitude during the summer. Begin at Camp Rock Campground and hike along the Beartrack Lakes Trail until you reach the lakes. See the hiking section for details on the hike. Brooks and Cutthroats predominate in these lakes.

CHEESMAN DAM

Location: South Platte. Take Highway 285 south to Pine Junction. Turn south onto County Road 126 for 21.9 miles and park in the lot on the north side of the road. You can also park at Wigwam Campground, 1/3 mile west. Follow the Gill Trail (marked) which leads you along the river toward Cheesman Dam.

The section of river, downstream from its confluence with the North Fork of the South Platte River, is classified as a gold medal water in Colorado. This designation means that it has a high quality aquatic habitat, a high percentage of large trout, and the potential for trophy trout fishing and angling success. The area just below the dam is the crown jewel of the South Platte. Fishing in this stretch can bring up Rainbow Trout 15-22 pounds, and there are 500 pounds of fish per surface acre.

> ## Wilderness on Wheels
>
> Unique in Colorado, WOW, as it is commonly called, maintains a 20-acre facility at the base of Kenosha Pass for handicapped users.
>
> From April to October, the area is open to wheelchair campers, fishermen, and hikers. There are shelters along the trails and elevated tent decks in the campsites for easy accessibility.
>
> The fishing ponds are stocked with trout and are boardwalk accessible. Reservations for the campsites are recommended.
>
> Wilderness on Wheels is located on Highway 285 near Kenosha Pass. Call 303-988-2212 for more information.

ECHO LAKE

Location: Mt. Evans. Take Highway 103 to Echo Lake.

A popular, accessible spot, Echo Lake sits at the base of the Mount Evans and has stocked Rainbow Trout.

EVERGREEN LAKE

Location: Evergreen.   Take I-70 to the Evergreen exit and follow Highway 74 into central Evergreen.

A mostly stocked lake, Evergreen Lake is another good choice for a place to bring the family for the day. Sit along the banks or take out your own float tube. Tiger Muskies and stocked trout can be caught here. Ice fishing is also popular on this lake in the wintertime.

GOLF

EVERGREEN'S PUBLIC GOLF COURSE

Location: 29614 Upper Bear Creek Road, Evergreen, CO.   Next to Evergreen Lake.

Phone: 303-674-6351

Situated in the center of Evergreen, just off the lake, this 18-hole course dates back to the 1920s and is the only public golf course in the area.   Interestingly, this course is run by the City and County of Denver and is less expensive for Denver residents. Prices for Denver residents range from approximately $11 for nine holes to $14 for 18 holes on the weekends. For those outside of Denver, including residents in the area, the prices range from $13 for nine holes to $19 for 18 holes. It's open 6 a.m. to 6:30 p.m. from late April to mid-October, weather permitting. The clubhouse serves up breakfast, lunch, and dinner with traditional pub fare. Golf carts and club rentals are available at the pro shop, and lessons are offered by appointment.

Scenic swinging at Evergreen's Public Golf Course in the center of Evergreen.

K. Blum

HIWAN GOLF CLUB
Location: 30671 Club House Lane, Evergreen, CO
Phone: 303-674-3366 or the pro-shop: 303-674-3369
   A private 18-hole course in Evergreen. The club offers a swimming pool and tennis courts as well.

OLD WEST DRIVING RANGE
Location: 14771 Highway 8, Morrison, CO
Phone: 303-697-8867
   Open most of the year, weather permitting, this range lets you practice driving a bucket of 70 balls for $5, and 115 balls for $7. Old West rents clubs and is open from 7 a.m. to 10 p.m. seven days a week. Mondays, it opens at 11 a.m.

RED ROCKS COUNTRY CLUB
Location: 16234 W. Belleview Avenue, Morrison, CO
Phone: 303-697-8008
   This private club offers a sweeping panorama of the Rocky Mountains along with 18 holes of manicured greens. They also have a clubhouse, swimming pool, and tennis courts.

HIKING

   A hiking mecca is what the local paper called the greater Evergreen area, and many who live here can attest to that. It's no wonder this region has earned that nickname with nine Jefferson County Open Space Parks between its borders and two national forests, wildlife refuges, and Denver Mountain Parks completing the picture. Whether you are just out for a short stroll under the pine trees, an educational venture, or an accelerated climb, you'll find what you are looking for in the foothills, and from Denver, it won't take you long to find that escape.
   There are several guides geared toward hiking to help you find your way. See the bibliography. National Forest Service offices also have topographic maps and trail information. The **Clear Creek Ranger District**, which manages Arapaho National Forest, is located in Idaho Springs on the road to Mt. Evans (101 Chicago Creek Road, Idaho Springs, CO, 303-567-2901). The **South Platte Ranger District**, which manages Pike National Forest, is located on Highway 285 just southwest of Indian Hills (19316 Goddard Ranch Court, Morrison, CO, 303-275-5610). Open space trail maps are found at the entrance to each open space park and are included here as well. If you want to get involved with a good group of mountain-loving folk, check out the **Colorado**

Mountain Club. The CMC is the premier hiking club in the Rocky Mountain region and is stationed nearby in Golden. They offer many different activities from hiking to canoeing and are also involved with conservation and educational programs. You can reach them at 303-279-3080.

For a day hike, you'll want to bring at least a water bottle (some open space parks have water; don't ever drink from the streams), rain gear, a snack, and extra clothing. Remember that in the summer, afternoon storms can interrupt what started as a leisurely hike, so start early and be prepared. To minimize the hassle of getting ready for a hike, it might be helpful to keep a daypack ready with all the above essentials for each member of your party. Sometimes just the thought of getting everybody out there along with the necessary equipment is overwhelming, and so it's good to keep prepared supplies on hand.

Also, always let someone know where you are going. Some of the trails have trail registers, but tell a friend or family member where you are going. With these precautions and ten essentials, you'll help guarantee a safe enjoyable outing.

The following trails provide a diverse range of terrain, wildlife, flowers, and vistas. Dogs are allowed on the trails as long as they are leashed. Day trips are listed first, followed by longer trails where you can romp for a day or even overnight. As with many of the activities in this chapter, there's a lot more out there to explore, so use this information as a starting point. The time listed under each hike is an approximate round-trip time for an average hiker.

> ## For an extended hike, always carry the ten essentials:
>
> Clothing
> Extra food and water
> Flashlight
> Fire starter
> First aid kit
> Pocket knife
> Nylon cord
> Space blanket or poncho
> Sunglasses and sunscreen
> Waterproof matches

RATING:

Easy: Anyone can do it. Great with children
Moderately Easy: A bit more rigorous, but still accessible to most hikers.
Moderately Difficult: Challenging because of its distance or elevation gain. With plenty of time, any level of hiker could also manage this rating.

DAY HIKES

BERGEN PEAK
See the mountain biking route for details. Allow 1/2 day.

CHIEF MOUNTAIN TRAIL
Distance: 3 miles round-trip
Rating: Moderately Easy
Time: 1 hour 15 minutes
Location: Arapaho National Forest. Take I-70 west to the Evergreen exit. Follow Evergreen Parkway to Highway 103 near Bergen Park. Head west on Highway 103 and go 13.1 miles, about four miles past the Arapaho National Forest marker to a pull-off area on the right side.

Chief Mountain offers a quick trip to a rocky summit with a 360-degree view of the Continental Divide and the plains. Although you steadily climb up this trail, it's not a hard climb and the trail is easy to follow. The treeless summit in an alpine environment feels like a climb to some of the fourteeners in the area and is just as rewarding. Once you park in the pull-off area, cross the road and look for a small marker with a trail that winds uphill. Once uphill, you'll see a white post with number 290, and then the trail becomes easier to follow. You'll continue, cross Squaw Pass Trail (see the skiing section), and ascend to the summit. Be cautious of summer storms since at the 11,709-foot summit you're exposed to wind, lightning, and hail. Return the same way.

The Chief Mountain Trail is a short climb into an alpine environment with 360-degree views.

K. Blum

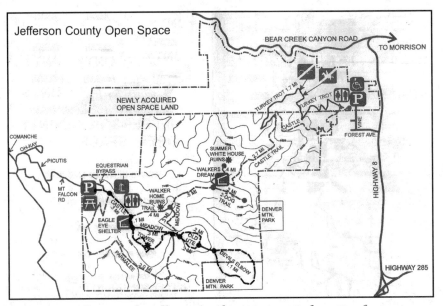

The Devil's Elbow Trail in Mount Falcon Park

DEVIL'S ELBOW TRAIL
Distance: 3.5 miles round-trip
Rating: Easy
Time: 2 hours 30 minutes
Location: Mount Falcon Park. Take Highway 285 to the Parmalee Gulch Road/Indian Hills. Follow Parmalee Gulch Road to Picutis Road. Follow the signs to Mount Falcon Park. This is the west entrance of the park; the other entrance is located in Morrison (see the mountain biking section).

Mount Falcon offers nice walks for all ages of hikers with awe-inspiring views and a chance to see hawks, wildflowers, and a bit of history. The Devil's Elbow Trail begins as the Castle Trail from the parking lot and travels through meadow and forest from shelter to lookout with great views of snow-capped peaks and the sprawling metropolis of Denver. Take the Castle Trail to the Meadow Trail and Eagle Eye shelter. At this shelter, you'll find several picnic tables and great views of the mountains, and usually you'll see circling hawks. From there, travel up the Tower Trail to another lookout, this one with views of Denver. Continue to the Old Lute Trail and finally the Devil's Elbow Trail, which loops around for more views. You'll pass close to a stone quarry, and it gets loud during weekdays. From there, loop back to the Meadow Trail and go through the meadow to the Walker Home Ruins where John Brisben Walker, a famous entrepreneur, once had his home. The walls and fireplace still remain. You can continue on east another 0.9 miles to Walkers' Dream, a site where Walker laid the groundwork for a summer home for the U.S. presidents. Or, you can continue back west on the Castle Trail to the parking lot. There are shorter variations of this trail. See the map.

EAGLE'S VIEW
Distance: 4 miles
Rating: Moderately Easy
Time: 3 hours
Location: Reynolds Park. Take Highway 285 south past Conifer to County Road 97 (Foxton Road). Head south about four miles to the first parking lot in the park.

As the name implies, from the top of this hike, you've got a bird's eye view all the way down to Pikes Peak. It's a good, get-away-from-it-all, yet accessible mountain climb. From the parking lot, take the Elkhorn Interpretive Trail right to the Raven's Roost Trail. Climb steadily all the way to the top. On the way down, take the Oxen Draw Trail for a change of pace. The Elkhorn Interpretive Trail is interesting in itself and is close to the picnic area. This park is also the only open space park in the area with a camping spot. Permits must be obtained to camp. Call Jefferson County Open Space at 303-271-5925.

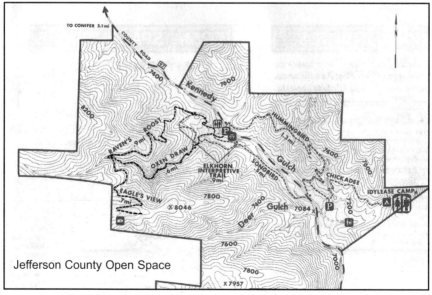

The Eagle's View Trail in Reynolds Park

GOLDEN WATERSHED*

Distance: 6000 acres to explore
Rating: Easy
Time: Varies
Location: Intersection of Highway 103/Squaw Pass Road and Old Squaw Pass Road. Take I-70 to the Evergreen exit. Follow Evergreen Parkway to Highway 103 near Bergen Park. Take Highway 103 toward Mt. Evans 4.3 miles to Old Squaw Pass Road. Take a right and parking area is on your left. There is another entrance 6.9 miles from the Highway 74/103 junction on Highway 103.
*This area is open for hunting between the last week of August and mid-November

What's different about this area is that it's primitive. Several trails and jeep roads crisscross the area, and you can use these established trails or wander through the meadows and forests. Tread lightly and bring a compass. The Division of Wildlife established this land as a hunting parcel, but during the spring and summer months, it's a great place to explore on foot. From the first parking area, a trail leads to a small reservoir and dam. It's only about ten minutes to the reservoir and an easy walk down a jeep road. From there you can explore the rest of this pristine reserve. Access into this reserve is by foot or horseback only. Equestrians will also find this a nice parcel to explore.

K. Blum

Golden Watershed offers plenty of space for walking.

MAXWELL FALLS TRAIL
Distance: 0.5 miles
Rating: Easy
Time: 30 minutes. Take more time to spend at the falls.
Location: Arapaho National Forest. Take I-70 to Evergreen. Follow Evergreen Parkway to Evergreen's center. Turn right (south) on Highway 73 and follow this until Brook Forest Road. Take Brook Forest Road 5.2 miles to a parking area and trailhead on the left, past the Brook Forest Inn.

Along the way to the upper trailhead for Maxwell Falls, you'll see a parking area for a hiking/mountain biking trail which is one possibility for beginning this hike. However, the trail is not too exciting, and because the main attraction is the falls, proceed past this to a parking area and trail that is just minutes away from the falls. During the spring and early summer, Maxwell Falls is at its peak and is a good reprieve from the heat. The trail is easy. Don't expect a huge waterfall, but the water flows from between the rocks and makes a pretty picnic spot.

MEYER RANCH TRAILS
Distance: 2-5 miles
Rating: Easy and Moderately Easy
Time: 2 hours
Location: Meyer Ranch Open Space Park. Take Highway 285 toward Conifer. About 0.5 miles before Aspen Park is the turnoff for South Turkey Creek Road and Meyer Ranch.

There are a variety of loop trails in this open space park providing hikers of all abilities a good day in the woods. These trails are especially pleasant in the fall when aspens turn the trails golden or in early spring when wildflowers carpet the lower meadows. To hike to the upper trails which offer views of the surrounding areas, take the Owl's Perch Trail to the Lodge Pole Loop to the Sunny Aspen Trail up the Old Ski Run Trail. At the top is a quiet picturesque meadow, but be cautious of private land. All the trails are wide and well-groomed and make for an enjoyable mountain walk.

STAPLETON NATURE TRAIL*
Distance: 0.6 miles
Rating: Easy
Time: 1 hour (with stops at the interpretive signs)
*Interpretive trail, made in part for blind users
Location: Genesee Park. Take I-70 to the Chief Hosa exit and go north on Stapleton Drive for 1.2 miles or the end of the road. Road is closed and two parking lots are there.

Although it bears the name of Denver's former airport, this trail is nowhere near the city rush and is a unique trail made especially with blind hikers in mind. Along this short walk are interpretive signs in both Braille and written English, and there's a cord which runs the length of the trail for hikers to follow. There are still some rocks, small inclines and declines, so sightless hikers need to keep this in mind. For everyone, this trail is a great first trail in the area because it introduces you to the native foliage and wildlife. On a rainy summer afternoon, this trail is a perfect place to go and take the kids. There's tree cover and a wonderfully rich, green environment. Take your time, as the signs instruct, and enjoy using your five senses along this trail.

THE THREE SISTERS AND THE BROTHER

Distance: 4 miles round-trip
Rating: Easy
Time: 1 hour 30 minutes
Location: Alderfer/Three Sisters Park. Take I-70 to Evergreen. Follow Evergreen Parkway to town and turn right on Highway 73. Take Highway 73 to Buffalo Park Road (across from the Evergreen Public Library). Turn right or west and go 2.5 miles to the west entrance and parking lot.

This park is always inspiring with views of the distant peaks and a lush meadow and rock outcroppings. There are many different combinations of trails in the area, including the Evergreen Mountain Trail, which is listed in the mountain biking section. All the trails are fairly easy to hike, and they wind through strands of aspen and pine to great vistas and good relaxation spots. The trail to the Three Sisters and the Brother hits the two prime scenic lookout points in the park. From the parking lot, take the Bluebird Meadow Trail east to the Silver Fox Trail and head east or left again on this trail. Stay on Silver Fox until you reach the Ponderosa Trail and take this around the Three Sisters Loop. From the top of Three Sisters you get good views of Evergreen and rolling hills. Continue with a descent down the Three Sisters Trail until you reach the Ponderosa Trail again, and from there, head east where you'll get a chance to go up to Brother's Lookout. It's a short climb up and well worth it as you can see for miles and miles and there are plenty of places to grab a snack and enjoy the sun. On the way down you can take a number of trails. The shortest route is to head down the Ponderosa Trail back to the parking lot.

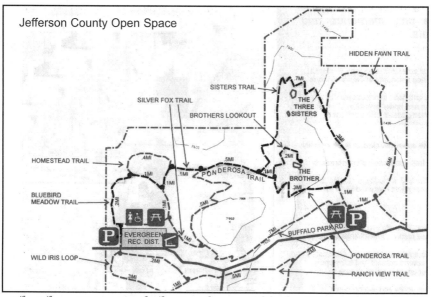

The Three Sisters and The Brother in Alderfer/Three Sisters Park

EXTENDED DAY HIKES/BACKPACKING

ABYSS LAKE TRAIL
Distance: 16 miles round-trip
Rating: Moderately Difficult
Time: 3 hours to Abyss Lake (one way)
Location: Mt. Evans Wilderness, Pike National Forest. To reach this trail, drive south from Bailey on Highway 285 11 miles to the town of Grant. Turn north onto County Road 62, the Guanella Pass Road. The trailhead and parking is 5.5 miles on the east (right) side of the road, south of Burning Bear Campground.

The Mt. Evans Wilderness area, so close to Evergreen, is a such a unique find along the Front Range, you'll want to return again and again. Nestled in a mountain bowl between Mt. Bierstadt and Mt. Evans, Abyss Lake provides a day of alpine scenery in this fantastic wilderness. Mountain goats and Bighorn sheep graze the rocky slopes around this 12,650-foot lake. From the parking lot, you'll follow the Scott Gomer Creek drainage and cross several small streams. Mt. Bierstadt comes into view about two miles along the trail, and you'll meander through the evergreen trees and the fresh mountain air. You'll meet up with the Rosalie Trail, but when the two divide, continue straight on the Abyss Trail in a northeast direction. After a series of fairly steep switchbacks, the trail will leave the trees and enter a willow grove close to a small lake. Follow the rock cairns to keep you on the trail. After another 1/2 hour, you'll cross the stream which drains from Abyss Lake and begin heading west across the tundra. These last several miles are above treeline. Keep an eye out for rock cairns to help you find the trail. Relax and enjoy a quiet alpine world.

BEARTRACK LAKES LOOP TRAIL*
Distance: 13 miles round-trip
Rating: Moderately Difficult
Time: 4-5 hours to Lower Beartrack Lake (one way)
Location: Mt. Evans Wilderness, Arapaho National Forest. To get there, take I-70 to Evergreen. Follow Evergreen Parkway to the lake. Turn west on Upper Bear Creek Road; continue for 6.3 miles; take a right which is really the continuation of Upper Bear Creek Road. Signs there point toward Singing River Ranch and Mt. Evans Outdoor Lab. Go for about 2 miles and stay right at next Y intersection. At second Y, take a left. Signs say State Wildlife Area and Mt. Evans Outdoor Lab. Go all the way to the main parking area, picnic ground; from there go right toward Camp Rock Campground (about 4.6 miles). It takes about 1/2 hour, a beautiful drive from Evergreen.
*open to hikers June 15-December 31

Another amazing hike in the Mt. Evans Wilderness, this loop is also a long day-trip and perfect for a multi-day backpacking excursion. From the lake, there are numerous possibilities for day hikes and fishing. To find the trail, if you're facing the campsites at Camp Rock, take the left trail, which is fairly easy to follow and winds its way along the creek for about a mile. After a mile, the trail begins to climb switchbacks and reaches a forest burn and corresponding views of the mountains. From there you'll re-enter the forest and meet up with the Cub Creek Trail which takes you to the turnoff for Beartrack Lakes. Although there are several trail signs along the way, follow the trail markings on the trees and take along the map as the path is sometimes not clear. On summer weekends, though, there are also usually plenty of people out on the trail to help you find your way.

Near the Lower Beartrack Lake is a campground with plenty of established camping spots. The lake is tucked into an alpine bowl at 11,200 feet with Rosalie Peak hovering above. For day hikes from there, try the climb up Rosalie Peak or the trails to Roosevelt or Upper Beartrack Lakes. To make the return trip, follow the trail back down and take the Cub Creek Trail left for several miles through an old burn, alpine environment, and more stunning views. At its junction with Beaver Meadows Trail, there is a quiet waterfall and small swimming hole for a refreshing dip. There are several campsites here as well. Once on the Beaver Meadows Trail, you'll pass several meadows with a good chance to see wildflowers and wildlife. With the trail mostly downhill from here, you'll soon arrive back at Camp Rock Campground. This trail is just one of many trails in this wilderness area suited for backpacking. Check out topographic maps of the area before you go. You can find them at the National Forest Service offices.

K. Blum

The Chicago Lakes Trail takes you into the wild high country in a day's walk.

CHICAGO LAKES TRAIL
Distance: 4 miles to lower Chicago Lake; 5.5 miles to upper lake (one way)
Rating: Moderately Difficult
Time: 4 hours round-trip to lower lake
Location: Mt. Evans Wilderness, Arapaho National Forest. Take I-70 to the Evergreen exit. Follow Evergreen Parkway to Highway 103 near Bergen Park. Take Highway 103 to Echo Lake and park in the parking area at the northwest end of the lake.

With a good tramp into the high country and its proximity to Denver, the Chicago Lakes Trail is worth a day trip. It could also be a jumping off point for other day trips up to some of the surrounding peaks, and thus makes a good backpacking spot. On weekends, many trail warriors have already discovered its appeal, and this serene destination becomes a buzz of activity. Try this trail on the off-seasons. Fall is beautiful with the aspen in their yellow glory. It's a fairly steady uphill climb to 12,000 feet, which accounts for its rating, but with enough rest breaks, anyone could do this. Begin at Echo Lake and follow the trail around the lake to the forested side. A trail on this side of the lake leads into the forest and isn't well-marked, but is well-trodden. From this trail, look right, and you'll see the trail marker to Chicago Lakes. The trail travels downhill to the creek with beautiful views of the upcoming mountains. After crossing the creek, you'll follow a jeep road up to the reservoir and then stay right on the road. You'll pass several cabins and then enter the Mt. Evans Wilderness. The trail here becomes more exposed as you pass through the 1978 forest burn. It's a steady climb up to the lakes, but once there you can relax, enjoy a lunch, or even go fishing. The upper lake is another climb and begins on the west side of the creek but is difficult to find. Ask other hikers while you are up there.

HORSEBACK RIDING

Most trails in the area are open to horses, and if you own your own horse, there are many places to explore. See the appendix for a complete listing of open space parks. Some of the longer rides can be found in the Mount Evans Wilderness Area, the Golden Watershed State Wildlife Area, along the Colorado Trail, and in the national forests. See the hiking section for details. For a guided trail ride, contact one of the following outfitters.

BEAR CREEK STABLES
Location: Bear Creek Lake Park, Morrison. Take C-470 to Morrison Road and go east a short distance to Bear Creek Lake Park.
Phone: 303-697-9666
People with any ability level and who are at least six years old can take these trail rides. Guides take you through Bear Creek Lake Park all year, weather permitting. Call to reserve.

WADE'S STABLES
Location: Bailey. Take Highway 285 south 1.5 miles past Bailey. Wade's is just off the highway. Look for the signs.
Phone: 303-838-7993
Guided trail rides take you through the Pike National Forest and private land. Any age and any ability can ride. Wade's is open seven days a week during the summer; spring and fall weekends; and during

the week in winter by appointment. Sleigh rides are also offered in winter.

HUNTING

Big and small game hunting is popular in the wilderness areas in this region but also strictly regulated by the Colorado Division of Wildlife. Anyone 12 or older needs a hunting license, and there are dates for each game season. Deer, elk, antelope, black bear, bighorn sheep, mountain goats, and mountain lions are found throughout the area. Both the Mt. Evans State Wildlife Area and Golden Watershed State Wildlife Area recently opened for hunters and provide good habitats for big game. For maps, brochures, rules, and regulations about hunting, call the **Colorado Division of Wildlife** regional office at 303-291-7227.

ICE SKATING

There's one place to ice skate in the area, and it's the only one you need. **Evergreen Lake** (Central Evergreen, 303-674-0532 or hotline: 303-512-9300) is the embodiment of outdoor ice skating—a large skating area, groomed every morning, with special rinks carved out just for ice hockey. If you haven't skated before, the lake is an easy one to learn on, and if you have skated before, you'll be hooked by this lake and pray for cold conditions. The lake usually opens around the area schools' Christmas break and stays open throughout the winter on evenings and weekends, weather permitting. Skates and hockey equipment can be rented, but it's easiest to bring your own. There is a charge for skating, and seasonal passes are available. Popular on weekends, so get there early or later in the day.

IN-LINE SKATING AND SKATEBOARDING

Rollerblading and skateboarding are a bit tougher here with the numerous dirt roads and rocky terrain. However, two places provide ample space to test and practice your skills.

C-470 BIKE PATH
Location: Take the C-470 exit to Morrison and head west about 1/8 mile to the parking lot at Morrison and Rooney Road. From there, head north on Rooney Road just up a slight hill to where you'll see the concrete path begin on your right.

This path, which follows the east side of C-470, is concrete and offers good ups and downs and some sharp turns. This is the same path listed above for bikers, and many people walk the path as well, so try and stay in control!

EVERGREEN SKATE PARK
Location: Evergreen Park and Recreation District, 5300 S. Olive Road, Evergreen. To find the park, take Highway 73 from the center of Evergreen to Buffalo Park Road. Turn right and continue until you reach the high school at S. Olive Road. Take a left and park in the Recreation Center's parking lot. The skate park is just up the hill.
Phone: 303-674-6441

Opened in August 1997 to the delight of many kids and located just west of the Evergreen Recreation Center, this park might just be one of the best in the metro area with its variety of jumps and obstacles. Both rollerbladers and skateboarders are required to wear safety equipment, and a minimal fee is charged. During school hours, the park is open 3 to 8 p.m. weekdays and 10 a.m. to 8 p.m. weekends. During the summer, the park is generally open all day, every day.

MOTORBIKING

Any of the mountain roads are great for motorcycling, especially Bear Creek Canyon, but to play around or take out a dirt bike, there's a spot just west of C-470 on Rooney Road. Managed by the City of Lakewood, the **Thunder Valley Motorcross Track** is open to motorbikes and ATVs. Cost varies depending on the type of bike. The track is open during the summer from Wednesday through Sunday. After Labor Day, the track is only open Saturday and Sunday. To reach the track, take the Morrison exit from C-470 and head west to Rooney Road. Follow Rooney Road past the speedway to Alameda Parkway. Take a left and continue following Rooney Road north. It's about a mile from Alameda Parkway along the frontage road to C-470. Call 303-697-1003 for more information.

RACING

For both spectators and those who like life in the fast lane, **Bandimere Speedway** in Morrison is unique along the Front Range. In addition to championship professional drag racing, the speedway is open for test nights and participation events. There is a drag racing series for kids, an "All-American High School Drag" just for teenagers, and truck, motorcycle, and go-kart racing. Events take place from April through October. Admission for participants ranges, but is generally around $35; admission for spectators ranges from $7 to $50, depending on the event. To reach the speedway, take the Morrison exit off C-470 west to Rooney Road. Bandimere Speedway is at 3051 S. Rooney Road. For more information, call the 24-hour hotline (303-697-4870).

RAFTING

Although most people head to the Arkansas River to experience whitewater thrills, Clear Creek, which runs through Idaho Springs, has some of the most challenging rapids per mile in the state. The key is to hit the right season, and during May and June, when water levels are at their highest, this river can't be beat. **Clear Creek Rafting** offers beginning, intermediate, and advanced full-day trips on Clear Creek. They also guide trips down the Arkansas River and into the Royal Gorge. Contact them for more information (303-277-9900).

Colorado Whitewater Photography

Clear Creek has some of the most challenging rapids in the state.

RODEO

Celebrating over 30 years in Evergreen, the **Evergreen Rodeo** is one of the biggest events of the summer in this area. Held in June each year at the El Pinal rodeo grounds, this last small-town, outdoor, professional rodeo in the metro area boasts world-class contestants along with multiple other fun activities. A parade, live music, dance, and barbecue are some of the festivities. Admission to the rodeo is $6 for adults, $4 for children, and free for children under age six. Take Stagecoach Road in Evergreen (near the new Albertsons) east about 0.5 miles to the grounds at the corner of Bronco Road.

SKIING

Although some of the nation's best downhill skiing is within an hour of the Denver, backcountry skiers will find great snow pack in the areas around Mt. Evans. Backcountry skiing allows you to escape from the downhill ski traffic and congestion at the resorts. You get to explore quiet trails, try out telemark turns in fresh powder, and as in the case of Mt. Evans, take terrific downhill runs...free. Once you strap on some skis and hit the backcountry, it's hard to go back to the crowded, expensive ski areas!

Novices can get a good taste of backcountry skiing in this region. For the trails listed here, you'll need a single or double-cambered ski with full metal edges. Waxless skis, with fish scales, are easier to manage. If you already have a pair of cross-country skating or race skis, by all means, use those. Then, once you get the "bug" for the backcountry, you might want to invest in skis with full metal edges.

Advanced skiers will meet their challenge on Mount Evans. For this run, downhill skis are just as good as telemark or mountaineering skis. Other advanced trails are nearby, but check out one of the good backcountry ski books for details. See the bibliography section for recommended reading.

Avalanches are one of the greatest dangers to the backcountry skiers. Every year, people die in avalanches, and many face close escapes. If you've ever seen an avalanche, it's something you'll never forget; you'll be thankful you're still alive. Mt. Evans is the only run here with avalanche danger, and you can not even attempt it until spring when snow is consolidated. Despite the lack of avalanche danger on the novice trails, if you're heading out into the backcountry, learn avalanche safety. The **Avalanche Information Center** has a 24-hour hotline from

November to April and offers various classes throughout the metro region (303-236-9435 for a recorded message during the season; 303-371-1080 for other information). REI in Lakewood offers some seminars, and there are several good books on the subject in the bibliography. Be informed.

You can rent skis at **Canyon Cycles** (26289 Highway 74, Kittredge, CO, 303-670-2728); **Paragon Sports** (2962 Evergreen Parkway, Evergreen, CO, 303-670-0092); or **Foothills Ski & Bike** (25948 Genesee Trail Road, Golden, CO, 303-526-2036).

Bring along a map, layers of clothing, and good sun protection, and you'll be ready to hit the trail. In addition to the trails listed here, try any of the open space parks when the weather is right. See the appendix.

Avalanche Awareness

There are several facts you should know in order to evaluate avalanche danger, but nature is unpredictable. Take a class or read more about avalanches before heading into the winter mountains. When choosing a route, the safest one is usually on ridgetops and slightly to the side where the wind is coming from and away from those beautiful whipped snow precipices called cornices. Out in the valley, away from the bottom of slopes, is your next best option. Call the avalanche hotline before you go and obey all signs. Carry an avalanche transceiver with you, a probe, and a collapsible shovel.
The Avalanche Hotline: 303-236-9435

Cold temperatures will maintain an unstable snow pack and, hence, be more prone toward slides.
Eighty to ninety percent of avalanches occur shortly before, during and after storms. Be cautious when snow has fallen quickly and there's at least six or more inches of new snow.
The first rapid, sustained warm-up of spring can cause avalanches. Fatalities from avalanches have occurred into July.
Leeward slopes (slopes that face away from the wind) may be more dangerous due to unstable wind slabs.
Most avalanches occur on slopes of 30 to 45 degrees, but may occur on slopes from 25 to 55 degrees.
Snow on north-facing slopes may take longer to stabilize, yet south-facing slopes are dangerous during the spring thaw.

NOVICE TRAILS

BURNING BEAR TRAIL*
Distance: 3.7 miles to the ridge summit
Time: 1/2 day-3/4 day
Location: Take Highway 285 south past Bailey to the town of Grant. Then head north on County Road 62 toward Guanella Pass 4.9 miles. The trailhead is on the west side of the road (left) on top of the switchbacks, marked with a cross-country skier symbol.
*Intermediate highlight

Most of the winter this trail has good snow pack because of its elevation (starting at 9,600 feet and reaching 10,850 feet) and because of its tree cover. From the trailhead, go northwest through an open meadow and cross the bridge over Geneva Creek. Continue along the western edge of the creek until you reach a fork, marked with a post. Tak a left (turn west), and you'll gradually climb as you ski along Burning Bear Creek. After about 2.5 miles, you'll come to an old log cabin, and this is a good turnaround point. **Intermediate highlight**: From here, the trail heads 1.2 miles into switchbacks to the top of the ridge and the summit of the trail. Keep an eye open for the blue diamond markers.

The greater Evergreen area has many quiet trails with easy access.

K. Blum

FAIRPLAY NORDIC CENTER
Distance: 22 kilometers of groomed trails
Time: Varies
Location: Fairplay. Take Highway 285 south to Fairplay. Take Main Street (Highway 9) in Fairplay to Fourth Street. Drive four blocks to a three-way intersection. Turn left and follow Beaver Creek Road 1.5 miles to the Nordic Center.
Phone: 719-836-2658

Although just beyond the scope of the area, the Fairplay Nordic Center is worth a mention for its great groomed trails. Named best cross- country ski center in Colorado, even with minimal snow pack, these trails provide satisfying skiing. There are trails for the beginner and challenging trails for the advanced skier. In fact, many ski racers use this area for their training. Day rates are very reasonable, and there is rental gear available.

IDAHO SPRINGS RESERVOIR
Distance: 6 miles round-trip
Time: 1/2 day
Location: Take I-70 to Idaho Springs. From Idaho Springs take Highway 103 toward Mt. Evans. Go nine miles and park on the right-hand side of the road at the Idaho Springs Reservoir sign.

For the beginner and intermediate skier, the trip to Idaho Springs Reservoir leads to a pleasant ski on a wide trail climbing 980 feet. Popular on the weekends, this might be better attempted during the week. Follow the trail through a lodgepole pine forest two miles to Camp Schwader which is gated and private. Ski to the right of this gate, past the horse stable and to the reservoir.

SOUTH CHICAGO CREEK TRAIL*
Distance: 4 miles round-trip
Time: 1/4 day
Location: Take Highway 103 from Idaho Springs almost nine miles. Park 200 yards below the Idaho Springs Reservoir sign on either side of the road.
*Intermediate/Advanced highlight

With an access similar to the Idaho Springs Reservoir, this is another fine trail. With a slow elevation gain of 800 feet, this trail offers plenty of opportunity for practicing backcountry ski techniques. You'll pass summer cabins, cross a river, and at 1.5 miles encounter a junction with a sign for "South Chicago Creek Trail" to the left. Stay right and continue for about 0.5 miles to the end of the trail and small clearing which makes a good lunch stop. **Intermediate/advanced highlight**: At the junction at 1.5 miles, take the left fork and head up the South Chicago Creek Trail. The trail is steep and narrow and ends at 11,000 feet.

SQUAW PASS TRAIL
Distance: up to 4 miles one way
Time: 1/4-1/2 day
Location: Mt. Evans. Take Highway 103 from Bergen Park toward Mt. Evans. There are four access points to this trail, and all are rather obscure. During winter weekends, there are often cars at the different points which will help point the way. At about 10 miles up Highway 103, begin to look for pull-offs and a trail heading up the bank of the south side of the highway. You can drop one car off here. Then, continue approximately another four miles. If you get to the picnic areas of Mt. Evans, you've gone too far. This last access point is on the left-hand side where there is parking and an old road which heads uphill.

For a fun, smooth descent, check out this trail off the road to Mt. Evans. The trail is an old road which parallels the newer road and is wide and often snow-covered throughout much of the season. From the parking area, ski up the road on the south side of the street. Soon, you'll meet a trail running east-west, and this is Squaw Pass Trail. Head downhill. If you continue up the road you're on, there are also other areas to explore.

ADVANCED TRAILS

MOUNT EVANS
Distance: 1.4 miles
Time: 1/4 day
Starting elevation: 14,120 feet
Downhill: 1,300 feet
Avalanche danger: Extreme. Wait until spring!
Location: Take Highway 103 from either Bergen Park or Idaho Springs all the way to the Mt. Evans Road. Take the Mt. Evans Road to the summit.

With a car shuttle, this spring descent rivals any downhill ski resort run. With an almost 45-degree slope, this run quickly tests even the advanced skier's skills. Do not attempt this unless you're confident about your skiing ability. The descent starts from the top of Mt. Evans, and so you'll have to wait until the road to the top opens, usually in early June. On the way up, stop at summit lake and survey the scene on the mountain. Once on the top, park in the lot and look for other skied tracks. There is a large main snowfield along with other options. If you hit this run right after the road opens, you could ski all the way to Echo Lake.

SLEDDING

There are three good, well-known sledding hills in the area, but many others if you look around. For Colorado snow, saucers, toboggans, and tubes work the best. Often, Flexible Flyers just sink right into the powdery snow.

BELL PARK
Location: Evergreen. From downtown Evergreen, take Highway 73, 1.8 miles to a pull-off on the south side of the street where the road makes a wide curve.

Close to Evergreen, this hill is a smooth, short ride, not too fast, but fun.

MEYER RANCH
Location: Aspen Park. Take Highway 285 south toward Fairplay. In the town of Aspen Park, Meyer Ranch is on the left.

A quarter mile from the parking lot is a popular sledding hill, and you'll see saucers and sleds flying when there's good snow. You can also walk farther up the trail for more of a ride. The ride down is not too steep, perfect for children.

PENCE PARK
Location: Indian Hills. Take Highway 285 to the Parmalee Gulch Road, Indian Hills exit. Travel about 4.5 miles to the hill just past Pence Park.

This hill in Indian Hills is a blast when snow conditions are right. With a quicker downhill than Meyer Ranch, this slope often forms small moguls form which leads to some air time while sledding.

Sledding in Pence Park is high-flying fun.

K. Blum

SNOWSHOEING

This popular and easy sport can be done anywhere in the mountain area. Any of the hiking trails, with enough snow cover, easily become snowshoe hot spots. Check out the open space listing in the appendix for parks that seem suited for snowshoeing. The area at the top of Guanella Pass is a fantastic wide open play area for snowshoe exploring. To find this area, drive to Georgetown or Grant and take County Road 62, Guanella Pass Road.

SWIMMING

K. Blum

A cool reprieve from summer's heat at Big Soda Lake beach.

BIG SODA LAKE
Location: Morrison. Take Highway 285 to the Morrison exit and turn east to Bear Creek Lake Park.
Phone: 303-697-6159

From May-Labor Day, Big Soda Lake is open for swimming. The only fee is the daily park pass which is $3 per vehicle, and for entertaining children, it's a real bargain. There is a sand beach, playground, concession stand, and small swimming area at the lake.

EVERGREEN RECREATION CENTER
Location: 5300 S. Olive Road, Evergreen. Take Highway 73 from the center of Evergreen to Buffalo Park Road. Turn right and continue until you reach the high school at S. Olive Road. Take a left and continue until the end of the road.
Phone: 303-674-6441

They provide all levels of lessons, a swim team, public swimming, and lap swims.

INDIAN SPRINGS RESORT
Location: 302 Soda Creek Road, Idaho Springs. Take I-70 to the Idaho Springs first exit and then follow the signs to the Indian Springs Resort.
Phone: 303-989-6666

Indian Springs has a natural warm mineral swimming pool open year-round from 9 a.m. to 10 p.m. They also have hot springs—see the Attractions chapter for details.

O'FALLON PARK
Location: Kittredge. Take Highway 285 to Parmalee Gulch Road or the Indian Hills exit and go all the way to its end in Kittredge. From there go east about 0.3 miles to the park which is on the south side of the street.

If you just want to dip your feet in or play in some cool mountain water, Bear Creek, which runs through Evergreen, offers those possibilities. Probably the best place to do this which is O'Fallon Park with numerous picnic areas and room for splashing.

TENNIS

Although there are several private facilities in the area, the public tennis courts are at the **Evergreen Recreation Center, Parmalee Elementary School** in Indian Hills, and **Evergreen Middle School**. During the school year, tennis teams practice at some of these places, so call 303-674-6441 to check on availability. No fee is charged.

WATER-SKIING

LITTLE SODA LAKE

Location: Morrison. Take Highway 285 to the Morrison exit and turn east to Bear Creek Lake Park.

Phone: 303-697-0121

Hours: Mondays and Fridays:10 a.m. to dusk; Tuesday-Thursday: noon until dusk; Saturday, Sundays, and holidays: 9 a.m. to dusk. Children's classes: Tuesday, Wednesday, and Thursday mornings.

Cost: $17 for 10 minutes or $95/hour.

Offering a chance to get out on skis for the first time or to hone your skills, this lake offers skiing by the Soda Lakes Water-ski School only. You access the lake through Bear Creek Lake Park, so a $3 entrance fee is required. Sessions include instruction and demo skis. You can buy the sessions in bulk at discount or rent the lake for a private party for $95/hour. Once you hone your skills, you can try some of their advanced boards, double skis, or knee boards. Westword, Denver's weekly paper, voted this the "Best Water Skiing Lake" in the area. It's a thin, long lake and a good change of pace from all of the land activities.

Chapter Five
Restaurants

Imagine dining in a warm adobe building and looking out at the great plains of Denver. Lights twinkle from the houses far below, a fire is burning in the fireplace, mandolin music wafts through the room, and your hot elk steak arrives. Or picture yourself in a comfortable Victorian home relaxing to classical music, eating a wild green salad, and drinking a fine glass of cabernet during a quiet conversation. Or, perhaps you and a group of your friends have gone out to dinner for your 40th birthday. The atmosphere is loud, festive, and you toast with award-winning margaritas.

The Greater Evergreen area has a wide range of restaurants from which to choose, from Mexican to Scandinavian and eclectic to elegant. Choices range from fun restaurants for families to romantic places for two. In fact, there are too many restaurants to name. What follows is a sampling of the area's best restaurants. Some are the author's favorites, while others are long-established places. With the area's growth, more restaurants are certain to arrive, so keep your eyes open.

For dinner in the area, you'll pay an average of $15/plate, with some exceptions. For lunch, expect an average of $7/plate. Evergreen is a casual place, so a pair of jeans and T-shirt are usually acceptable attire. Parking is easy, and even in winter you can usually reach every dining establishment. Just drive cautiously on the mountain roads after a night out.

The prices below represent approximate dinner plate prices. Addresses, meals served, hours, prices, credit cards, reservations (if recommended), and type of cuisine are listed for each restaurant. Before heading out for the evening, you might want to confirm the restaurant's hours. At the end of this section, bakeries, coffee shops, and pizza take-out options are listed along with addresses and phone numbers. To find a restaurant by type of cuisine or price, consult the appendix.

Per person dinner plate prices

$ Under $10
$$ 10-20
$$$ 20-30
$$$$ 30 and up

Credit cards accepted

All=Accepts all the following:
Visa=Visa
MC=Master Card
Amex=American Express
Disc=Discover
DC=Diner's Club

DINING ESTABLISHMENTS

THE BISTRO
6830 Highway 73
Evergreen, CO
303-674-7670
Meals Served: Dinner
Hours: Sunday-Thursday: 5-9 p.m.; Friday-Saturday: 5-10 p.m.
Price: $$-$$$
Credit Cards: Visa, MC, Disc
Reservations: Recommended on weekends
Type of Cuisine: Fresh American/Californian

Housed in an old log building with log-beamed ceilings, soft lights, wood floors, and a large stone fireplace, this restaurant breathes mountain atmosphere. Voted best restaurant in Jefferson County, The Bistro serves up amazing food in a noisy, but intimate atmosphere. World music—mandolin, flamenco, and jazz—provides the background on weekend nights. During cooler mountain evenings, a fire helps warm the room, and you gaze out the windows at the snow falling on pine trees. Yet, in addition to atmosphere, the cuisine is mouth-watering and beautifully prepared. Excellent and unique to the mountain area is The Bistro's selection of tapas: portobello mushrooms sautéed with garlic and butter, steamed mussels, lobster and brie in a puffed pastry with champagne sauce. It is as good as it sounds. For entrées, they offer fresh fish, a Colorado game selection, and filet mignon. Definitely save room for dessert. Their preparation and quality of ingredients is some of the best around.

BUCK SNORT SALOON
15921 Elk Creek Road
Pine, CO
303-838-0284
Meals Served: Lunch and dinner
Hours: Every day: noon-9 p.m. (kitchen is open)
Bar stays open until 11 p.m. weekdays; midnight on weekends
Price: $
Credit Cards: Checks and cash only
Type of Cuisine: American

Pine's Buck Snort Saloon has won the *Rocky Mountain News'* polls for "Best Place to Take an Out-of-Town Visitor," "Best Mountain Bar," and "Best Out-of-the-Way Burger" for many years. Personally, I would add Best Out-of-the-Way Burrito to that list. Of course, for greater Evergreen area dwellers, this place isn't so out of the way. The drive there is spectacular, and the restaurant/bar is wedged between the rocks of Sphinx Park, known to climbers all over the world. It's also convenient to the South Platte River, some of the best fishing in the state. The Bucksnort isn't fancy—could it be with such a name?—but it's the genuine thing with wooden décor and booths, writing all over the walls, and a pool table up front. There is live music on the weekends too. You feel miles away from any city when you're back here, and the food fills you up nicely after a good day of recreation.

CHART HOUSE
25908 Genesee Trail Road
Golden, CO
303-526-9813
Meals Served: Dinner
Hours: Monday-Saturday: 5-10 p.m.; Sunday: 4:30-10 p.m.
Price: $$-$$$
Credit Cards: Visa, MC, Amex, DC
Reservations: Recommended on weekends
Type of Cuisine: Steak and seafood

Popular with locals and Denver residents, the Chart House continues to dish up some of the largest servings of fresh seafood and steaks around. The salad bar at this place might be the largest you've ever seen and even includes caviar. Request a seat near the windows, which look out on Denver, and come dressed in casual clothes with a good appetite. It's a moving, busy place with people coming, going, and talking, and food arriving sizzling hot at your table. Most of the items are grilled and cooked to perfection. Their specialities include prime rib and Chart House Mud Pie.

COAL MINE DRAGON
Safeway Center, Conifer, CO, 303-838-7870
Lakepoint Center, Evergreen, CO, 303-670-1341
Meals Served: Lunch and dinner
Hours: *Conifer* Every day: 11 a.m.-9 p.m.
         Evergreen Monday-Thursday: 11 a.m.-9:30 p.m.; Friday-
         Saturday: 11 a.m.-10 p.m.; Sunday: 4-9 p.m.
Price: $
Credit Cards: Visa, MC
Type of Cuisine: Chinese

Convenient for take-out Chinese food, the Coal Mine Dragon now has two locations serving the greater Evergreen area. Although they have the same name, each one is independently owned. They offer reasonable Chinese food, reasonably priced. The Conifer location is a bit dark, but the Evergreen one is lighter, just off the lake, and convenient for après ice-skating eating. Quick take-out seems the way to go.

CONEY ISLAND
Highway 285
Aspen Park, CO
303-838-4210
Meals Served: Breakfast, lunch, dinner
Hours: Every day: 9 a.m.-9 p.m.
Price: $
Credit Cards: Cash and in-state checks only
Type of Cuisine: American

Built in 1966 during an architectural craze of restaurants constructed to replicate the food they served, Coney Island is the big hot dog you see on your way up Highway 285. You can't miss it. It was first established on Colfax Avenue in Denver as part of a larger chain, but it wasn't successful. Later, a couple named the Slagers bought it and moved it to Aspen Park. Of course, there was some protest when residents woke up one morning in 1970 to find a large hot dog in their backyards. But the restaurant quickly became a favorite and remains one today. It's American all the way. Hamburgers, hot dogs, french fries, shakes, chicken breast sandwiches, breaded fish, and sausage egg biscuits for breakfast are all served quickly and at unbelievably low prices. It has to be the cheapest food in the area, and it's really decent, especially the thick shakes and crisp thick fries. Stop on your way to work or up into the mountains, and you'll find yourself returning again and again.

It's hard to miss Coney Island in Aspen Park.

K. Blum

DICK'S HICKORY DOCK
26220 Highway 74
Kittredge, CO
303-674-9612
Meals Served: Lunch and dinner
Hours: Sunday-Thursday: 11:30 a.m.-9 p.m.; Friday-Saturday: 11:30 a.m.-10 p.m.
Price: $$
Credit Cards: Visa, MC, Amex, Disc
Reservations: Taken for parties of 10 or more; come early to get on the waiting list.
Type of Cuisine: Barbecue

People magazine has voted this one of the country's top 10 barbecue restaurants, and it's definitely one of the most delightful barbecue locations around. Situated on Bear Creek, Dick's Hickory Dock has been a local institution since 1977. During the warm months, the crowds come here to taste the slow-hickory-smoked ribs cooked in the "Bubba" pit smoker. And they come to eat under the pine trees along Bear Creek. There are outside picnic tables and inside seating in a restored log cabin with windows on all sides. Their sauce, used on all the meats, is mild and sweet, and the ribs are cooked to perfection. Dick's also serves up steak, fish, large burgers, and even vegetarian choices. For vegetarians, the barbecue tofu is really supreme. Expect a long wait at Dick's on weekends, but there's plenty of bench space and friendly folk.

DREAM CAFÉ
102 Market Street
Morrison, CO
303-697-1280
Meals Served: Breakfast, lunch, and dinner
Hours: Closed Mondays; Tuesday-Wednesday: 11 a.m.-4 p.m.; Thursday-Friday: 11 a.m.-9 p.m.; Saturday: 8 a.m.-9 p.m.; Sunday: 8 a.m.-8 p.m.
Price: $-$$
Credit Cards: Visa, MC
Reservations: Recommended for dinner and for large groups
Type of Cuisine: Fresh American/Californian

The Dream Café in Morrison is a relaxing treat anytime.

K. Blum

As the name suggests, this restaurant is quiet and relaxing. With new age, classical, and folk music playing in this restored Victorian home, along with the soul-nourishing food this place serves, you can't help but come out feeling rejuvenated. It's like aromatherapy or a few hours at a spa. For breakfast, lunch, and light dinners, they serve panini topped with eggs, salmon and lox, or fresh vegetables and feta cheese, just to name a few. The Dream Dips that they serve—spicy black beans and hummus, artichoke and creamy red pepper, spinach and onions—can become a healthy addiction. Soups and salad dressings are homemade with the freshest ingredients. Dinner entrées which change weekly, usually include a fresh seafood dish, Thai stir fry, and chicken, beef, and vegetarian dishes. All come with warm bread, salad, and veggies or pasta. Their wine is handpicked, and they feature microbrews from all over Colorado. Dream Café is a treat.

EL RANCHO VILLAGE
29260 Highway 40
Golden, CO
303-526-0661
Meals Served: Lunch, dinner, Sunday brunch
Hours: Monday-Thursday: 10:30 a.m.-9 p.m.; Friday-Saturday: 10:30 a.m.-10 p.m.; Sunday: 9 a.m.-2 p.m.; 3-9 p.m.
Price: $$ (lunch averages about $7.50)
Credit Cards: Visa, MC, Amex, Disc
Reservations: Recommended on weekends
Type of Cuisine: American/Western

For the best views around of the Continental Divide, try this window-full dining room. At 7,686 feet above sea level and conveniently located, El Rancho has served over four million guests in its long history. Built in 1948 and remodeled recently, the dining room is large, sunny, and feels like a ski lodge. It has been selected as one of the 500 leading restaurants in the United States and is a great place to take out-of-town visitors to show Colorado alpine scenery. El Rancho serves up western food—buffalo, roast chicken, and steak, along with their specialty, dry aged beef. All entrées are served with house salad, fresh vegetables, potato, or delicious cinnamon rolls upon request. There is a bar here, and they brew their own beer. On winter weekends, the place is often a hub for the aprés-ski crowd.

THE FORT
19192 Route 8
Morrison, CO
303-697-4771
Meals Served: Dinner
Hours: Monday-Friday: 5:30-9:30 p.m.; Saturday: 5-9:30 p.m.; Sunday: 5-8:30 p.m.
Price: $$$-$$$$
Credit Cards: All
Reservations: Recommended
Type of Cuisine: American/Western

How does one explain this famous establishment that Greater Evergreen area residents are lucky to have in their backyard? The world leaders ate here during the Summit of the Eight, which was held in Denver in 1997; people get engaged here; anniversaries and birthdays are celebrated here; and out-of-town guests are brought to The

Fort to get a taste of Colorado cuisine and to see the lights of Denver. It's the place to go for a special occasion, and if you haven't been yet, make plans soon. The Fort is an all adobe structure made to authentically resemble Colorado's first trading post. The inside is warm, decorated with Native American artifacts and oil paintings. Outside in the courtyard, there is often a bonfire burning. From the window tables, you can look out at Denver's lights twinkling below. The food is amazing! Taste Rocky Mountain oysters here or any of the wild game entrées like elk, quail, rattlesnake, or buffalo. During the weekends, and often during the week, it gets packed, but it's a fun and lively place and an absolutely awesome dining experience.

HOG HEAVEN
12 Rosalie Road, Highway 285 (Crow Hill)
Bailey, CO
303-838-8814
Meals Served: Lunch and dinner
Hours: Closed Monday, Tuesday, and Wednesday; *March-December* 11 a.m.-8 p.m.; *Memorial Day-Labor Day* 11 a.m.-9 p.m.
Price: $
Credit Cards: Cash and in-state checks only
Type of Cuisine: Barbecue

Get a slab of ribs to go or relax in this little roadside attraction that has been drawing people for years. They serve up platters of spare ribs, beef, pork, hot links, and sausage the traditional barbecue way with white bread, coleslaw, and potato salad or baked beans. For dessert, they have fresh fruit cobblers and sweet potato pie. There's not much to this roadside venue, and just a few picnic tables for eating, but it's simple, genuine barbecue. Look for the red caboose on the top of Crow Hill to find it.

ITALIAN TOUCH
Safeway Center
Conifer, CO
303-838-6069
Meals Served: Lunch and dinner
Hours: Monday-Friday: 9 a.m.-9 p.m.; Saturday-Sunday: 9 a.m.-10 p.m.
Price: $-$$
Credit Cards: Visa, MC, Amex, Disc
Type of Cuisine: Italian

Simple and unpretentious, the Italian Touch has good basic Italian fare for very reasonable prices. Their pizza is New York style, and you have a choice of thin, thick, or pan crust. A new pizza creation is their take and bake gourmet pizza. You take it home pre-made and bake it 15 to 20 minutes in the oven, and it's excellent pizza. Their sandwiches are made on homemade bread, and their garlic bread is homemade too. For a satisfying meal that won't break your wallet, stop by the Italian Touch.

J.WILLIAM'S CAFE
1193 Highway 74
Evergreen, CO
303-674-5967
Meals Served: Lunch, brunch, take-out dinners
Hours: Closed Mondays; Tuesday-Friday: 11 a.m.-2 p.m.; Saturday-Sunday: 9 a.m.-2 p.m.
Take-out: Tuesday-Saturday: 8 a.m.-7 p.m.; Sunday: 8 a.m.-3 p.m.
Price: $-$$
Credit Cards: Visa, MC
Type of Cuisine: Fresh American/Californian

Unique to the area in that it offers take-out meals as its primary business, J. William's serves up equally tasty brunch and lunch. What's great is that the take-out meals are a complete dinner, and within minutes, you are eating quality gourmet cuisine at your home. The menu varies. One day it may be a halibut and salmon pinwheels with asparagus bundles and basmati rice, and another day, tenderloin filet wrapped in apple-smoked bacon stuffed with wild mushroom stuffing. All are made with the freshest ingredients and served with a flair. For lunch and brunch, J. Williams offers a large selection of homemade soups and salads, pizza of the day, pastas, roasted chicken, soft fish tacos, and eggs, frittatas, homemade oatmeal, and fresh-squeezed orange juice. Their dining area is decorated in art nouveau style with tapestries on the walls and multi-colored bottles on the marble tables. They offer marvelous catering services and special order food from fresh fish to cheese and deli meats from around the world.

MORRISON INN
301 Bear Creek Avenue
Morrison, CO
303-697-6650
Meals Served: Lunch, dinner, and Sunday brunch
Hours: Monday-Saturday: 10 a.m.-11 p.m.; Sunday: 9 a.m.-10 p.m.
Price: $-$$
Credit Cards: Visa, MC
Reservations: For larger parties; come early on concert nights.
Type of Cuisine: Mexican

The Morrison Inn is a restaurant and bar with a casual attitude and a fun atmosphere. There's plenty of room at the inn, but it's always packed. People come for the award-winning margaritas and the eclectic Mexican meals. Fajitas are their specialty, and the tamales and burritos (especially the one that "Ate Juarez") are tasty. Old photos of Morrison and Native American rugs line the walls of this old adobe building. Upstairs is a large patio. Homemade potato chips are one of their choice side items, and of course, crisp chips and salsa (all you can eat) will keep you satisfied before your meal. Before a concert at Red Rocks or simply to celebrate life, this restaurant fits the bill.

Lori Hladik

Outside eating at the Morrison Inn, a popular spot before or after Red Rocks concerts or anytime.

RIB CRIB
27905 Meadow Drive
Evergreen, CO
303-674-4633
Meals Served: Lunch and dinner
Hours: Monday-Thursday: 11 a.m.-10 p.m.; Friday-Saturday: 11a.m.-11 p.m.; Sunday: 11a.m.-10 p.m.
Price: $$
Credit Cards: Visa, MC
Type of Cuisine: American and Barbecue

The sweet barbecue marinade is excellent at the Rib Crib. It's homemade and is smothered on their meats and poultry, which are slowly smoked in applewood. They've got the typical barbecue fare— ribs, chicken, turkey, and ham—as well as sandwiches, salads, and soups. The inside is small and often smoky and works better as a bar, complete with pool table. There's an outside patio for warmer months.

RIVER SAGE
4651 S. Highway 73 (corner of Main Street)
Evergreen, CO
303-674-2914
Meals Served: Breakfast, lunch, brunch, dinner
Hours: Closed Tuesday; Monday-Friday: 7 a.m.-9 p.m.; Saturday.-Sunday: 7:30 a.m.-9 p.m.
Price: $$
Credit Cards: Visa, MC, Amex
Reservations: Recommended on weekends
Type of Cuisine: Fresh American/Californian

People have called this cuisine, "Exuberant Rocky Mountain Cuisine." Translated, that means an eclectic mix of food prepared with style and care. The restaurant tries to live by the River Sage legend which tells of an old wise man who lived a tranquil life along Bear Creek and gave inspiration to others. The cuisine and atmosphere of this restaurant provides nourishment for the body and soul. It begins with a mystical and homey décor with soft lighting, many plants, new age music, and of course, the creek, which flows right outside the door. A steaming cup of River Sage Spice tea served in inspirational pottery mugs will bring you further into the atmosphere, followed by a hearty breakfast, lunch, or dinner. The lemon tahini house salad dressing is so good it's been bottled and sold. Some of the special dinner items include an Indonesian vegetable dish and many grill items served with a variety of sauces ranging from ginger garlic teriyaki to lemon garlic cilantro. There are often acoustic concerts here on the weekends.

THE ROUNDUP GRILL

28215 Highway 74/Main Street
Evergreen, CO
303-674-3173
Meals Served: Breakfast, lunch, dinner every day
Hours: Monday-Friday: 7:30 a.m.-9 p.m.; Saturday: 9 a.m.-9 p.m.;
Sunday: 9 a.m.-8 p.m.
Price: $$
Credit Cards: Visa, MC, Amex, Disc
Type of Cuisine: American/Western

Critically acclaimed by locals and tourists, this western-style eatery serves up hearty fare as well as a glimpse of the past. Old saddles and ranching implements decorate the walls, as do photos and newspaper clippings of old town Evergreen. The cuisine is typical Colorado fare. For breakfast, there's steak and eggs, huevos rancheros, and burritos. Their lunch menu ranges from large salads to fried shrimp and sandwiches. Dinners, accompanied by fresh melt-in-your-mouth biscuits with sweet Chimayo butter and soup or salad, are generously portioned and satisfying. Prime rib, elk medallions, baby back ribs and fresh trout are just a few of the choices. Try the grilled chicken molé which has won awards in the metro area. On several weeknights, the restaurant features live jazz and acoustic guitar.

THUY HOA OF EVERGREEN

28080 Douglas Park Road
Evergreen, CO
303-674-5421
Meals Served: Lunch and dinner
Hours: Closed Mondays; Tuesday-Thursday: 11 a.m.-2:30 p.m.; 5-9 p.m.; Friday-Saturday: 11 a.m.-2:30 p.m.; 5-10 p.m.; Sunday: 12-2:30 p.m.; 5-9 p.m.
Price: $$
Credit Cards: All
Type of Cuisine: Vietnamese

This Evergreen establishment serves up fresh and plentiful Vietnamese fare. With over 100 dishes on the dinner menu, Thuy Hoa appeals to those seeking light Asian cuisine for the vegetarian or the carnivore. The atmosphere is airy. Windows stretch the length of the walls; high ceilings and plenty of light complete the picture. Meals are hearty and fresh. A combination appetizer, for example, is served with a full dish of grilled meats, delicately spiced, with another overflowing plate of vegetable greens and herbs. Dishes include typical Vietnamese Phõ (noodle bowls), exotic dishes of crispy duck, Five Spice Grilled Quail, and garlic and lemongrass frog legs.

TIVOLI DEER
26295 Hilltop Drive
Kittredge, CO
303-670-0941
Meals Served: Lunch, dinner, Sunday brunch
Hours: Closed Tuesdays; Monday-Thursday: 11 a.m.-2:30 p.m.; 5:30 p.m.-9 p.m.; Friday-Saturday: 11a.m.-2:30p.m.; 5:30 p.m.-10 p.m.; Sunday: 10 a.m.-2:30 p.m.; 5:30 p.m.-9 p.m.
Price: $$-$$$$ (lunch averages $9)
Credit Cards: All
Reservations: Yes, on weekends
Attire: Semi-formal attire on Saturday night
Type of Cuisine: Continental

The Tivoli Dinner offers first-class cuisine in a Scandinavian setting.

Lori Hladik

One of the best and most unique dining experiences in the area, the Tivoli Deer always gets rave reviews. There is both a casual and formal dining room, and a Saturday night out here is a dining experience. Saturday is a set menu and expensive, but well worth the price. You are treated to a four-course meal served with the house wine and a touch of elegance. Your entrée choices range from Breast of Long Island Duckling to Kotelet of Pork. For dessert, you can indulge in the infamous Coupe Denmark, a combination of Ghiradelli chocolate and vanilla ice cream with roasted almonds over a baked meringue shell. In addition to Saturday dinner, they serve a reasonably-priced lunch menu with the same gourmet flair and a wonderful champagne brunch. Dinner during the rest of the week is also excellent, and the atmosphere is relaxing and comfortable.

TONY RIGATONI'S PIZZA AND PASTA
215 Highway 74 (Main Street)
Morrison, CO
303-697-5508
Meals Served: Lunch and dinner
Hours: Monday-Thursday: 11:30 a.m.-9 p.m.; Friday-Saturday: 11:30
a.m.-10 p.m.; Sunday: noon-9 p.m.
Price: $-$$
Credit Cards: Visa, MC
Reservations: No reservations taken, but call ahead for the waiting list.
Type of Cuisine: Italian

This Italian eatery, located on Main Street in Morrison, has the
biggest calzone you have probably ever seen or tried to eat. For its
price, the Calzone Abbondanza is definitely the bargain on the menu.
If you're hungry, go for it; if not, you have leftovers for several days.
Eating outside on the patio is nice on warm evenings, and this is a
good spot to take the kids. All the dinners of typical Italian fare are
large and come with salad and bread. During the summer or nights of
Red Rocks concerts, call ahead to get on the waiting list.

WHIPPLETREE
1338 County Road 65
Evergreen, CO
303-674-9944
Meals Served: Lunch and dinner
Hours: Monday-Saturday: 11 a.m.-10 p.m.; Sunday: 11 a.m.-9 p.m.; bar
stays open longer
Price: $
Credit Cards: Visa, MC
Reservations: Recommended on weekends and for larger parties
Type of Cuisine: Mexican

For everyone on the north side of the Evergreen area, this restaurant is your choice for Mexican cuisine. Most items are your traditional Mexican dishes, but they've added some unique ones such as
the fluenas (corn shells with chicken, cream cheese, and chile strips),
Albondigas soup, and appetizers like stuffed mushrooms with Alaskan
pollock and snow crab in brandy-champagne tarragon sauce topped
with Swiss cheese. Fajitas here are also very good and served with
fresh tomatoes, lettuce, and excellent guacamole. The food seems
pricey for Mexican, but it's good and always attracts the crowds.

WILDFLOWER CAFE

28035 Main Street
Evergreen, CO
303-674-3323
Meals Served: Breakfast, lunch, dinner, brunch
Hours: Monday: 11 a.m.-2 p.m.; Tuesday: 7 a.m.-2 p.m.; Wednesday-Saturday: 7 a.m.-9 p.m.; Sunday: 7 a.m.-8:30 p.m.
Price: $ (Lunch and breakfast average $5-6.)
Credit Cards: Visa, MC
Reservations: Come early on weekends for breakfast/lunch; dinner reservations recommended.
Type of Cuisine: American and Southwestern

Everyone knows your name at the Wildflower Café, a local eatery.

Lori Hladik

Quickly becoming an Evergreen institution, the Wildflower is friendly, comfortable, and serves tasty fare. Everything is casual. If you go there often enough, the owners and wait staff will know your name and your interests. Children's photos, autographed photos, children's napkin doodles, and many photos of the Queen (one of the owners is British) decorate the walls. Mornings are bustling times with people eating at every available spot: outside, on the sidewalk, and once, they even served a breakfast to a party on the back of a pickup. There are typical American breakfasts and brunches with some added healthy touches like their Wild Leaf Omelette, Turkey Dill Crepes, or Bowla Granola. They serve up incredible skillet selections, fresh juices, coffee, and brewed immune-boosting or stomach-ease teas which are refilled just like a hot cup of coffee. Lunches are tasty sandwiches, burgers, and a selection of fresh salads. For dinner, the Wildflower offers what they call a "Global Menu," which includes an array of dishes from different countries. Spinach manicotti, a tuna jerk sandwich, and curry chicken breast are a few of the items, and most come with very tasty sides like garlic mashed potatoes.

BAKERIES

ALPINE PASTRIES
3877 Highway 74, Evergreen, CO, 303-674-2120
  Variety of baked goods.

THE BAGELRY
1242 Bergen Parkway, Evergreen, CO, 303-674-1413
  Hot bagels, muffins, fresh salads, espresso, and soups.

BAILEY'S BLAZIN' BAKE SHOP
25997 Conifer Road, Aspen Park, CO, 303-838-0421
  Just off Highway 285 in Aspen Park. Assorted fresh pastries, muffins, scones, and monster cinnamon rolls. Homemade pies, gourmet coffees, and smoothies. Lunch items too.

THE DONUT SHOPPE
Main Street, Evergreen, CO, 303-674-2151
  Yummy donuts, muffins, and bagels, espresso and hot drinks.

GARY & CHERYL'S GOODIES
101 Bear Creek Ave., Morrison, CO, 303-697-1061
  Delicious baked goods, cinnamon rolls, breads, and ice cream.

MORRISON GROCERY
311 Highway 74, Main Street, Morrison, CO, 303-697-4336
  World leaders took this cheesecake back to Europe with them after the Summit of the Eight.

ESPRESSO

BUFFALO MOON
Genesee Towne Centre, Golden, CO, 303-526-7675
Espresso brewing for the morning commuter along with steaming assorted teas. Many quaint mercantile items for sale.

THE COFFEE CABIN
289125 Main Street, Evergreen, CO, 303-670-2050
Pleasant pastel interior. Espresso, hot drinks, and gift items.

COFFEE SHACK
10698 Highway 285, #B, Conifer, CO, 303-838-9353
Drive-thru coffee. Variety of coffee and cold drinks.

COMMON GROUND COFFEE
26289 Highway 74, Kittredge, CO, 303-670-8433
A nice simple place to grab a hot cup of joe and a pastry. Also serves lunch items.

CUP & CHAUCER
10875 Highway 285, Conifer, CO, 303-816-0016
Small, cozy. Hot drinks, espresso.

EVERGREEN COFFEE SHOP
28055 Main Street, Evergreen, CO, 303-679-8663
Located inside the restored Evergreen Hotel. Wooden décor, antique tables, and couches. Fresh breads and pastries, coffee, chai.

THE GROUND UP
Lakepoint Center, Evergreen, CO, 303-670-8623
Close to Evergreen Lake and a good warm-up after ice skating. Espresso, teas, panini sandwiches, and a selection of world foods.

INDIAN HILLS ESPRESSO
5510 Parmalee Gulch Road, Indian Hills, CO, 303-697-6825
Friendly atmosphere serving breakfast, lunch, and some dinners. Coffee the way you like it. Relaxing room and local gifts for sale.

XPRESSO DRIVE THRU
Bergen Village Shopping Center, Evergreen, CO
Open for the morning commute and a quick drive through.

PIZZA

BELLA'S PIZZA
Evergreen North Center, Evergreen, CO, 303-674-2223
Chicago-style pizzeria with dining, carry out, take-out and delivery.

DOMINO'S PIZZA
30901 Stagecoach Boulevard, Evergreen, CO, 303-674-3030
Delivery or carryout.

GUIDO'S PIZZA
25948 Genesee Trail Road, Golden, CO, 303-526-1510
Pizza, sandwiches, calzones, salads. Dine in or carry out.

J.J. MADWELLS
26412 Main Street, Conifer, CO, 303-838-1440
Italian food and real New York pizza. Spinach pizza with double crust
is their specialty. Eat in, dine out, delivery. Patio, beer, wine.

LITTLE CAESARS' PIZZA
3897 Evergreen Parkway, Evergreen, CO, 303-674-1100
Take-out.

PIZZA ETC.
#1 Delwood Drive, Bailey, CO, 303-838-5354
Take-out only. Thick or thin crust pizza, sandwiches, calzones, and
baked goods.

PIZZA HUT
31226 Lewis Ridge Road, Evergreen, CO, 303-674-1907
Dine in, carry out. Also offers a lunch buffet (Monday-Friday).

POPPIES
6941 Highway 73, Evergreen, CO, 303-674-1007
Pizza, stromboli, dinner specials, sub sandwiches to go. Also serves
breakfast and espresso.

TOMMY'S PIZZA
King Soopers Center, Bergen Park, CO, 303-679-0538
Take and bake pizza and ready-to-eat pizza. Lunch with pizza by the
slice and Italian subs.

Chapter Six
Lodging

From the mid-1800s when Thomas Bergen first settled in the area and welcomed traveling miners, the greater Evergreen area has been known for its accommodations. In the early 1900s, an abundance of resorts provided lodging to Denverites who wanted to escape the city heat and find serenity in the mountains. Evergreen and the Platte Canyon were established as a summer resort community and housed more residents in summer than in winter. Denver residents also bought up land in surrounding communities, such as Indian Hills, and built summer cabins. These small communities under the evergreen trees bustled with summer visitors.

Troutdale-in-the-Pines, built in the early 1900s, was probably the biggest and most celebrated hotel in the area. Although originally established as a small-scale resort with cabins, a small hotel, and lake, the resort blossomed by the mid-1900s into a four-story hotel able to house 300 guests, with tennis courts, a golf course, a fine dining establishment, and a dance hall. Famous visitors such as Greta Garbo and Teddy Roosevelt came to the foothills during those days.

Since that time, resorts such as Bendemeer, Greystone, Kiowa Lodge, and Singin' River Ranch have come and gone, leaving their mark on the history of this area. Many other still remain, though, and under new owners are embracing the past through renovations and remodeling. The visitor today will not find the colossal Troutdale-in-the-Pines, which became defunct in the 1960s, but will discover other originals such as the Brook Forest Inn and Marshdale Lodge (now the Bears Inn, a bed and breakfast). Guests will also find a variety of smaller inns, lodges, cottages, cabins, and bed and breakfasts which all offer a unique mountain experience.

A Quality Inn will be moving into town, just outside Bergen Park near El Rancho Village, the first chain hotel in the area. More inns are sure to follow, so keep your ears open. For now, though, the following is this area's selection of accommodations for the business traveler, family vacation, or romantic getaway.

USEFUL INFORMATION

ADDRESS

Address, including zip code is given, so that you can correspond with the inn. Many of the places now have a website or e-mail, and this is also listed. Places between Morrison and Evergreen along the I-70 corridor have a Golden address.

DIRECTIONS

Directions are given from Denver. With many places, there are different ways to get there. Most lodges are easy to find

RATES

Summer is no longer the only season visitors come to this area, and the accommodations listed are open all year. Some rates vary depending on the season, but due to the popularity of winter sports and the mild winters in Colorado, many of the lodges keep their rates consistent year-round. To find a lodging option by price, consult the appendix. Because prices are always changing, the following is a price guideline to show approximately how much the lodge costs. When you call to make reservations, please confirm the price.

$ 60-75

$$ 75-100

$$$ 100 and up

ACCOMMODATIONS AVAILABLE

Whether it's a one bedroom, a cabin, large houses, etc...this listing should give you a brief glance at what the lodge has to offer.

CREDIT CARDS

The following are symbols you will see for credit cards accepted. Some lodges accept checks as well. Ask when you call for reservations.

All=Accepts all the following

Visa=Visa

MC=Master Card

Amex=American Express

Disc=Discover

DC=Diner's Club

DISCOUNTS

Some lodges offer senior discounts, long-term stay discounts, or AAA discounts. If the inn offers a discount, it is listed.

MINIMUM STAY

Unlike inns of the past, many of the lodges now do not require a minimum stay. There are a few that retain this policy, and these places are marked in the introductory section.

CHILDREN

Many of the lodges welcome children, and if they do, this is also marked in the introductory section.

PETS

Many of the lodges do not accept pets. If they do, this is also marked in the introductory section to each one.

SMOKING

With most lodges, you can smoke outside the buildings, and sometimes that means right out your front door. **If** smoking is allowed in the rooms or cabins, this is marked in the introductory section. There are only a few that allow smoking inside.

BREAKFAST

If the lodge offers breakfast, this is marked in the introductory section. For bed and breakfast inns, this meal is described in the narrative for each entry.

LODGING

The Abundant Way Chalet rooms are located on the grounds of an old estate.

K. Blum

THE ABUNDANT WAY CHALET
4980 Highway 73
Evergreen, CO 80439
303-674-7467
Directions: Take I-70 west from Denver and exit at Evergreen Parkway. Follow Evergreen Parkway until you get to Evergreen. Turn right or south on on Highway 73 at the stoplight in Evergreen and go 0.5 miles. The Abundant Way is on the east side of the street, next to the Evergreen Public Library.
Rates: $$-$$$
Accommodations available: Two cabins with two bedrooms, three suites, one with two bedrooms, and two guest rooms

Credit Cards: Visa, MC, Amex
Minimum stay: Three days in summer (cabins only)
Children: Welcome
Pets: Discretionary
Meeting room available

 This lodge, located close to Main Street Evergreen, is a good place to stay with families or for a romantic getaway, since there are a variety of room choices. All rooms have private entrances, private baths, and the majority of them have fireplaces. One has a private hot tub. All are situated on the grounds of a 1930s estate. The grounds are landscaped and pleasant with picnic areas and grills. Cabins include full kitchens, and all rooms are bright, sunny, and well-decorated. If in a romantic mood, try the "Enchanted" room. For a family vacation, check out one of the cabins.

ASHLEY HOUSE BED & BREAKFAST

30500 Highway 40
Golden, CO 80401
303-526-2411 (metro Denver) 1-800-308-2411
Directions: Take I-70 west from Denver and exit at Evergreen Parkway. At the first traffic signal, turn right or west and travel 0.3 miles on Highway 40. You'll cross back over I-70. Ashley House is on the left and has a steep driveway.
Rates: $$
Accommodations available: Five rooms
Credit cards: Visa, MC, Amex, Disc
Discounts: 10% for reserving entire house; extended stay discount
Children: Welcome
Breakfast: Full breakfast

Ashley House is a comfortable modern home with views of the Continental Divide.

Courtesy of Ashley House

This modern bed and breakfast is one of the newest accommodation in the area and offers the comforts of a modern home. The bedrooms in the three-story home all have private baths, TV, and VCR. Hosts Ken and Tim have stocked the home with a large selection of movies. There is a main room where guests can mingle and relax in front of the fireplace, a game room, and a deck with a hot tub and an inspiring view of the mountains. Breakfast is served every morning, and the fare is typical American: biscuits, bacon, eggs, French toast, and fruit.

A good short-term housing option or summer retreat, Bauer's Spruce Island Chalets are situated on a park-like setting.

K. Blum

BAUER'S SPRUCE ISLAND CHALETS
5937 S. Brook Forest Road
Evergreen, CO 80439
303-674-4757
www.BSIChalets.com
email: info@BSIChalets.com
Directions: Take I-70 west from Denver and exit at Evergreen Parkway. Follow Evergreen Parkway until you get to Evergreen. Turn right on on Highway 73 at the stoplight in Evergreen and go two miles to Brook Forest Road. Turn south and go 1.1 miles to Bauer's Spruce Island Chalets which is on the right. You can also take Highway 285 to Conifer and then head north toward Evergreen. You'll see Brook Forest Road on your left. Go 1.1 miles to the lodge.
Rates: $-$$$ depending on number of guests
Accommodations available: Two studios, two 1 bedrooms, one 2 bedroom, two 3 bedrooms, one 4 bedroom cottage
Credit cards: Visa, MC, Amex
Discounts: Pay for six nights, get seventh night free (off-season); pay three weeks, get fourth week free (off-season)

Minimum stay: Studios (two-night minimum) Everything else (four-day minimum)
Children: Welcome
Pets: Ok, with additional charge
Smoking: Allowed

These individual cabins, surrounded by national forest land, are a good choice as a short-term housing option or a summer retreat. There are a number of lodging options available from studios to a small four-bedroom house. Each place is clean with modern conveniences including cable TV. All but the studios (which have kitchenettes) have full kitchens. Cottages with two or more bedrooms have fireplaces. From linens to kitchen utensils, everything you need is included here. There is a park-like setting surrounding the cabins with a stream, picnic tables, grills, and outdoor games and sports equipment available for use. Prices vary depending on size of accommodation and number of people, so be sure to call and ask for their brochure.

BEAR CREEK CABINS
27400 Highway 74
Evergreen, CO 80439
303-674-3442
Directions: Take I-70 west from Denver and exit at Evergreen Parkway. Follow Evergreen Parkway until you get to Evergreen. Continue east 3/4 of a mile. The cabins are on the south side of the road by the creek. You can also access the cabins from Indian Hills. Take Highway 285 to the Indian Hills/Parmalee Gulch Road Exit and go all the way to its end in Kittredge. From there, go west toward Evergreen on Highway 74 until you reach the cabins on your left or south side of the road.
Rates: $$
Accommodations available: Eight rooms in four separate cabins
Credit cards: Visa, MC, Amex
Discounts: Group rates; Orvis fishing discounts; weekly and monthly rates
Children: Welcome
Smoking: Allowed

This lodge, formerly called Davidson Lodge, has been hosting mountain visitors for 50 years, and it's a place people return to again and again. The cabins are the original log structures, remodeled throughout and large and comfortable. Each one has a rock fireplace, kitchen with dishes and cookware, TV, phone, wood for the fireplace, and coffee. All have queen-sized beds, and some have an additional double beds as well.

Just outside the cabin door is one of the main attractions, though, and that is Bear Creek, a fisherman's dream. Host Bruce is an avid fly fisherman and will rent you fishing equipment. Fishing is catch and release only and supreme, according to Bruce. The cabin property also runs adjacent to park land, so trailheads are accessible from this lodge. Bring your own food and make early reservations for this serene sweet spot on Bear Creek.

A taste of mountain living and charming history at the Bears Inn Bed & Breakfast.

Courtesy of the Bears Inn

BEARS INN BED & BREAKFAST
27425 Spruce Lane
Evergreen, CO 80439
303-670-1205 (metro Denver) or 1-800-863-1205
website: www.bearsinn.com
Directions: From Denver, take Highway 285 south toward Fairplay and exit at North Turkey Creek. Follow Turkey Creek to Highway 73 (it ends here). Turn right or north; the inn is 1/3 mile down on the east side of the street.
Rates: $$-$$$
Accommodations available: 11 rooms, including one suite
Credit cards: Visa, MC, Amex
Discounts: $10 less Sunday-Thursday (November-May 15th); 10% senior; 10% extended stay; 10% AAA discount; corporate programs
Minimum stay: Two nights on holidays
Breakfast: Full breakfast
Meeting Facilities available
Built as an inn in 1924 and run during the years as a resort, summer camp, lodge, and finally a bed and breakfast, this historic place has charm. As the name suggests, bears, whether teddy bears or quilted, are found throughout the inn.

Each room is uniquely decorated thematically, including wildflowers, Christmas, and an English fox hunt. Each room has a private bath, telephone with on-line access, and cable TV. In the great room, exposed log beams, hardwood floors, leather couches, a stone fireplace, and the hosts' golden retrievers give this inn a cozy mountain feel. A full country breakfast is served every morning, featuring homemade breads, plus their fruit and hot specialities.

Business travelers are able to use the office, which includes fax, phone, and copy machine. In fact, this lodge is a great place for a corporate retreat. Call about details. Special murder mystery nights are also held at the inn and include dinner at a neighboring restaurant (The Bistro), a wine and cheese party, lodging, and breakfast. For the business customer and the weekend-getaway guest, this inn offers a nice taste of mountain living.

BROOK FOREST INN

8136 Brook Forest Road
Evergreen, CO 80439
303-674-9919

Directions: There are two ways to reach the inn. Take I-70 west from Denver and exit at Evergreen Parkway. Follow Evergreen Parkway until you get to Evergreen. Turn right on on Highway 73 at the stoplight in Evergreen and go two miles to Brook Forest Road. Turn south on Brook Forest Road and go 5.1 miles to the inn on the left. Or, take Highway 285 south to Conifer. Turn north on Highway 73 and head toward Evergreen until you reach Brook Forest road. Turn south on Brook Forest Road and go 5.1 miles to the inn.

Rates: $-$$$
Accommodations available: 16 guest rooms (including three suites)
Credit cards: Visa, MC, Amex
Discounts: Winter rates available
Children: Welcome (extra cost)
Breakfast: Continental

An Evergreen landmark since the 1900s, the Brook Forest Inn has been an elite destination for Denver residents. Celebrities, including Harry S. Truman and Liberace, have visited the inn over the years, and stories have grown from ghosts having parties on the third floor to gold hidden in the walls.

Now completely renovated, the inn retains its original charm. Rooms breathe with an old Victorian décor and are richly furnished with European antiques. The majority have king-sized beds. All come with private bath, and most with Jaccuzzi tubs. Bathrobes, coffee, and overnight necessities are included with the price and pamper guests. There is often afternoon tea during the week and fresh fruits and chocolates before bed. A gourmet continental breakfast is served each morning with homemade muffins, fresh fruit, juices and coffee.

The Brook Forest Inn also boasts a formal dining room downstairs with elegant cuisine. Whether relaxing in the parlor room, listening to the baby grand piano, eating a world-class meal, or listening for the friendly ghosts, this inn offers an elegant, refreshing step back in history. The rates are high, but not unreasonable for the experience.

CLIFF HOUSE LODGE
121 Stone Street
Morrison, CO 80465
303-697-9732
Directions: From Denver, take C-470 to the Morrison exit. Take Morrison Road west two blocks, stay right at the Y (heading toward Red Rocks) and go two more blocks. You'll see the inn directly in front of you. It's in the quaint town of Morrison.
Rates: $$$
Accommodations available: Ten cottages
Credit cards: Visa, MC
Discounts: Weekdays

Walk into the courtyard of this old-style European inn, and you'll feel miles away from the rest of the world even though it's a minute's walk to downtown Morrison. The inn was built in 1873 by George Morrison as his family's home.

Each cottage has a private entrance and its own indoor or outdoor hot tub. The rooms are elegantly furnished with chandeliers, antiques, queen-sized beds, TV and VCR, and private bath. Some cottages have fireplaces and sitting rooms. All come with plush robes for the hot tub.

Romantic honeymoon or anniversary packages are available at this quaint mountain inn and include an elegant breakfast for two delivered

The cottages at the Cliff House Lodge are great for a romantic weekend that feels miles away from the rest of the world.

Courtesy of Cliff House Lodge

to the room and champagne on arrival. The cottages are pricey, but for a relaxing, romantic weekend, it's a find along the front range.

CRYSTAL LAKE RESORT/BED & BREAKFAST
29200 Crystal Lake Road
P.O. Box 529
Pine, CO 80470
303-838-5253
Directions: From Denver, take Highway 285 south toward Fairplay. Continue past Conifer 7.2 miles to Pine Junction. Turn left (south) at the traffic light onto County Road 126 (Pine Valley Road). Go six miles and look for the Crystal Lake signs. At the signs, turn right and continue until you reach the lodge.
Rates: $$-$$$
Accommodations available: Seven rooms
Credit cards: Visa, MC, Disc
Discounts: Group
Minimum stay: Two nights on summer weekends; three nights on holidays
Children: Welcome
Breakfast: Full

Crystal Lake has always been known as a fisherman's dream. In the 1880s, regular trains brought fishermen to the lake. In the 1920s, Charles Eggert bought the lake, founded Eggert Ice Company which supplied much of Denver's ice, and built the lodge. From the 1940s until 1972, the restaurant at the lake was a popular spot. And today, the resort is returning to its glory days.

Under new ownership, the resort operates as a bed and breakfast and grill restaurant. Adjacent to Pike National Forest and Jefferson County Open Space Parks, Crystal Lake is ideal for the recreation lover. Hiking, horseback riding, mountain biking, and of course, fishing are at your doorstep. Resort guests can also fish the lake without a license. However, for the 2.5 mile private South Platte River frontage, you will need a Colorado fishing license. The seven rustic guest rooms are close to the water. A hot breakfast is served each morning. Relax on the deck in the outdoor Jacuzzi, or experience the great outdoors at Crystal Lake.

EVERGREEN BED & BREAKFAST
1005 S. Linda Lane
Evergreen, CO 80439
303-526-5216
Directions: Take I-70 west from Denver and exit at Evergreen Parkway. Follow Evergreen Parkway one mile to Valley Road on the west side of

Evergreen Bed & Breakfast welcomes pets and is a comfortable overnight stay in the mountains.

Courtesy of
Evergreen Bed &
Breakfast

street (across from Kerr Gulch). Take Valley Road to Linda Lane. The Evergreen Bed & Breakfast is on the left side of the street.

Rates: $-$$
Accommodations available: Three rooms
Credit cards: Check and cash only
Discounts: Longer stay
Children: Welcome
Pets: Ok
Breakfast: Full

Convenient to I-70 and the mountain communities, this lodge is a relaxed home. With only three bedrooms, it's a small comfortable place. Host Ted does catering in the area, so breakfasts are filling and tasty. The bathrooms are shared, and the entire house is open to all, including an outside sun porch and downstairs kitchen complete with refrigerator, stove, and dishes. Ted has a dog and loves to host other pets as well. This place makes a good family stay, comfortable overnight in the mountains, or a good short-term housing option.

EVERGREEN LODGE
5331 Highway 73
P.O. Box 2861
Evergreen, CO 80437-2861
303-674-6927

Directions: Take I-70 west from Denver and exit at Evergreen Parkway. Follow Evergreen Parkway until you get to Evergreen. Turn right on Highway 73 at the stoplight in Evergreen and go two miles to Brook Forest Road. Evergreen Lodge is on the southwest corner of Brook Forest and Highway 73.

Rates: $$-$$$
Accommodations available: Ten rooms in cottages and chalet

Credit cards: Visa, MC
Minimum stay: Three days on summer weekends
Children: Welcome
Pets: On approval

This lodge offers a variety of options for a romantic getaway and comfortable suites for a retreat. Nestled in the pines along Cub Creek, the cottages and rooms in the lodge are decorated in traditional mountain décor with wood interiors, lodgepole beds, and wood-beamed ceilings.

Nine of the ten units have complete kitchens. Most have queen-sized beds, many come with a private outdoor deck, and some come with fireplaces. There is cable television in every room and complimentary tea and coffee. Outside, there's a children's playground, teepee, barbecue grills, and picnic tables.

THE HIGHLAND HAVEN

4395 Independence Trail
Evergreen, CO 80439
303-674-3577; 1-800-459-2406
www.highlandhaven.com

Directions: Take I-70 west from Denver and exit at Evergreen Parkway. Follow Evergreen Parkway eight miles. You'll go through Evergreen to reach Independence Trail on the right or south.
Rates: $$-$$$
Accommodations available: Seven cottages, five suites, and four guest rooms
Credit cards: All
Discounts: 10% senior AAA discount; 10% weekly stay discount
Minimum stay: Some cottages require minimum stay during peak seasons and holidays
Children: Welcome; under 12 stay free
Breakfast: Continental

Voted as one of the top three inns in Colorado in 1997, awarded a three-diamond rating from the American Automobile Association, and recipient of top honors from *Colorado Homes & Lifestyles*, The Highland Haven is well-known for excellent customer service and clean, elegant, mountain lodging.

This formal country inn sits adjacent to Bear Creek on beautifully landscaped grounds. It offers travelers, business people, and family vacationers a myriad of options. The four guest rooms are small with queen beds and private entrances. The five suites offer bedrooms, sitting rooms, kitchens, private decks, TVs and VCRs, and Jacuzzi tubs. The cottages have moss rock fireplaces, timber beams, and honey pine or canopy beds, and they are spacious and private. They also have kitchens; some also have wet bars, garden patios with grills, and TV, VCR, and CD players.

Relax for a weekend and enjoy the first-class service of the Highland Haven.

THE HORTON HOUSE BED & BREAKFAST
105 Canon Street
P.O. Box 223
Morrison, CO 80465
303-697-8526
Directions: From Denver, take C-470 to the Morrison exit. Take Morrison Road through town to the second stop light. Go left over a small bridge, then take a right (west). The Horton House is on the left.
Rates: $$
Accommodations available: Three guest rooms
Credit cards: Visa, MC
Discounts: 10% senior discount; 10% discount for families visiting relatives in the nursing home nearby.
Breakfast: Full

Built in 1870, this home has served as a family home, as Dr. Luce's horse and buggy practice, a Mexican restaurant, and finally as an inn. Lila, who now runs the bed and breakfast, grew up in this home and has retained treasured family heirlooms. The house, a quaint pink dwelling on Bear Creek, is packed with antiques and stories.

The backyard is well landscaped and shady during hot, dry summer days, and there is a sunroom on the back of the house, where Lila, an avid ballroom dancer, holds morning aerobics and evening Karaoke. Guest rooms all have double beds, cable TV, and private baths with showers.

Situated along Bear Creek in downtown Morrison, The Horton House is a relaxing weekend spot.

K. Blum

A full country breakfast is served every morning with fare from pastries to a special Texas casserole with spicy potatoes and eggs. This is a bed and breakfast experience that feels as if you are staying at grandma's home. You'll share the house with a cat and dog as well.

MEADOW CREEK BED & BREAKFAST
13438 US Highway 285 (Berry Hill Lane at Douglass Ranch)
Pine, CO 80470
303-838-4167
Directions: From Denver, take Highway 285 south toward Fairplay. From the Conifer Center, continue 5.3 miles on Highway 285. Take a left at Highway 285 Frontage Road (just past Elk Creek Road). Continue past the school and take the next left into Douglass Ranch. Follow the signs to Meadow Creek.
Rates: $$$
Accommodations available: Five rooms, one suite, one separate cottage
Credit cards: Visa, MC, Amex
Minimum stay: Two-night minimum on weekends
Breakfast: Full

Voted best Colorado lodge in 1997, Meadow Creek Bed & Breakfast is an enjoyable mountain experience.

Courtesy of Meadow Creek Bed & Breakfast

Another award-winning Colorado lodge, this bed and breakfast was voted the best in Colorado in 1997. Guests have called it the "do nothing lodge." Nestled in the pines, on 35 acres of land, this stone lodge is perfect. All rooms have private baths, and a Jacuzzi and sauna are open to all. Several of the rooms have their own Jacuzzi tub, including the cottage, which is a perfect haven of privacy. Outside hummingbirds flitter, and wildflowers bloom. There are plenty of places to roam on the spacious grounds. Inside, the rooms are cozy, and the smell of homemade pastries, breads, hashbrowns, and eggs permeates the air. This inn often fills up with repeat customers, so make your reservations early.

MOUNTAIN VIEW BED & BREAKFAST
4754 Picutis Road,
P.O. Box 631
Indian Hills, CO 80454-0631
303-697-6896

Directions: From Denver, take Highway 285 south toward Fairplay. Exit at Parmalee Gulch Road (Indian Hills exit). Go north 2.5 miles to Picutis Road (the turn-off for Mt. Falcon Park). Mountain View is the first home on the right and is marked.

Rates: $$-$$$

Accommodation available: Two guest rooms, one suite, one cabin

Credit cards: Visa, MC, Amex, DC

Children: Depends on availability

Breakfast: Full

Built as a writer's colony house in 1926, this country home has seen its share of history. The Richardsons, a German and British couple, have lived in the home since 1980 and began the bed and breakfast in 1995.

The two guest rooms and suite on the top floor of this home in the town of Indian Hills are large and furnished elegantly with European antiques. Guests have access to a large sitting room with wide picture windows that overlook the hills and mountain sunsets. The cabin with its private entrance is more modern, embraces a southwestern motif, and includes a dining area, private deck, Jacuzzi, and fireplace.

Hearty breakfasts are served each morning downstairs and include such specialities as cream-filled French toast, country-fried potatoes, mushroom and egg casserole, and fresh smoked Alaska salmon (the Richardson's son works in Alaska). In addition, an afternoon tea is served in the upstairs sitting room with homemade scones, cheese and chutney, and of course, hot tea. This inn is a nice escape.

Mountain View Bed & Breakfast is located in Indian Hills in a quiet mountain setting.

Courtesy of
Mountain View Bed
& Breakfast

WHITE BUFFALO LODGE
20056 Spring Creek Trail
P.O. Box 575
Pine, CO 80470
303-838-5301

Directions: From Denver, take Highway 285 south toward Fairplay. Continue past Conifer 7.2 miles on Highway 285 to Pine Junction. Turn left at the traffic light onto County Road 126. Go 13 miles through Pine and Buffalo Creek. Go 1/4 mile past new fire station south of Buffalo Creek. Turn left at Spring Creek Trail. Go 1.8 miles and White Buffalo Lodge is on the left in a subdivision called Spring Creek Ranch.

Rates: $$$
Accommodation available: Four rooms
Credit cards: Cash only
Discounts: Longer stay. Discounts without horses.
Minimum stay: Two nights
Breakfast: Full

Nestled into the pines bordering the Pike National Forest is this horse lover's bed and breakfast. Unique to the area, this lodge will treat you to a relaxing bed and breakfast experience while your horse is taken care of as well. Rates are for the price of two people and two horses. Every two horses are given their own private corral with salt, water, and plenty of hay.

Of the four rooms, one has a private marble bath and private deck; the other three share baths. The main room has a large TV, rock fireplaces, and videos, and there's a gourmet kitchen with supplies and a refrigerator. Breakfasts are all you can eat, hearty enough to get you ready for a day with your horse on the trail. If you don't have a horse, come to relax, mountain bike, fish in the gold medal waters nearby, or go hiking. The place is quiet, and you can even enjoy a massage from the host, a massage therapist. It's a unique getaway.

Come with your horses or by yourself to experience a mountain weekend at White Buffalo Lodge.

Courtesy of White
Buffalo Lodge

Chapter Seven
Celebrations

For many brides and grooms, the mountains just outside Denver are the perfect setting for a wedding. Whether it is in the middle of a meadow with elk grazing nearby, on a porch overlooking the city skyline, or in an historic lodge with a fire glowing in the fireplace, this area is home to an array of places to hold weddings, receptions, and parties.

There are 16 places to hold such celebrations in the area, but many more if you consider the mountain parks, restaurants, and small inns which sometimes allow you to get married on their lawns. I remember walking through one of the open space parks and coming upon a bride and groom who had just said their vows in a meadow bursting with wildflowers.

Although the following descriptions are geared toward weddings, many of the places hold corporate retreats, company Christmas dinners, memorial services, and wedding anniversary parties. If, in addition to weddings, any of these types of parties are the norm, they are listed under the description.

Remember that this information is just a beginning. If you really want to get married under the waterfalls at Maxwell Falls or say your vows on the stage of Red Rocks, inquire. In addition, remember to book early. Many of the places listed are filled during summer months and sometimes during the spring and fall at least a year in advance. Try choosing non-peak days, such as weekdays, and try a season other than summer. Winter is really a glorious time with light snow and some warm days, and all the roads are usually accessible.

In the first section are places that have their own chapels; one is only a wedding chapel. You can get married at any of the reception centers listed, but if you specifically want a chapel, try one of the first three places or try your local church.

USEFUL INFORMATION

ADDRESS

The address, with zip code, is listed so that you can correspond with the facility. Golden addresses are just off I-70.

SPACE AVAILABLE

This gives you the general space available. You'll want to visit the site to check this out further.

NUMBER OF PEOPLE

This information provides you with maximum numbers the facility can hold. If there's a question, or you're really set on having more people than the place suggests, call them.

PRICE AND SERVICES INCLUDED

Prices listed are approximate, usually based on a weekend night celebration. For different days of the week and different seasons, the price varies considerably at many of the places. Consider the price listed here on average as the highest you'll have to pay (as of the time of writing). Always call to double-check current prices.

TIME AVAILABLE

Sometimes, reception centers have time blocks they allow for weddings. At some sites, events need to be finished early in the evening because of neighbors or park regulations.

CATERING

"Hire own" or "Provided" is listed. If catering is provided, you'll have to use the facility's services. If it's not provided, many of the centers will give you recommendations.

LIQUOR

This depends on what type of license the facility has. Your options are cash bar, open bar, or bring your own. At some places, liquor is prohibited.

MULTIPLE EVENTS

Some places will hold two or more celebrations at once, and this is usually a consideration for most brides and grooms. At a few centers, this isn't a problem as they are large enough to support it. However, check this option if it is a concern and call the center to discuss it.

SPECIAL SERVICES

This section lists whether the reception center helps you plan your wedding or offers consultations. In addition, this is where you'll discover which ones also host many corporate parties.

DIRECTIONS

Although there are photos of many of the centers here, you might want to drive by and check out each facility.

RECEPTION CENTERS

BOETTCHER MANSION
900 Colorow Road
Golden, CO 80401
303-526-0855
Space available: One large room with adjacent patio; carriage house with adjacent patio; gazebo; conference rooms; bridal changing rooms
Number of people: 200 in the Fireside Room; 75 in the Carriage House; 20 in the Gazebo; 10 in the smaller conference rooms
Price and services included: *Fireside Room*: $350/hour; *Carriage House*: $175/hour; *Gazebo*: $50/hour
   Price includes rental of room, tables and chairs; rooms have minimum time requirements.
Time available: 8 a.m.-4 p.m./5:30 p.m.-2 a.m.
Catering: Hire own. Full kitchen available
Liquor: Open bar. Can't sell alcohol. Need continuous bar supervision and prior approval.
Multiple events: Yes
Special services: List of vendors, suppliers. Boettcher Mansion also does many corporate parties.
Directions: Take I-70 west from Denver and get off at the Lookout Mountain exit. Follow the signs to Boettcher and the Lookout Mountain Nature Center.

The historic Boettcher Mansion sits atop Lookout Mountain and offers an elegant summer home atmosphere.

K. Blum

This historic mansion, built in 1917, sits on Lookout Mountain with views of the Continental Divide and the Denver environs. A German-style façade, flower gardens, and nature trails greet you at the entrance to this mansion, and the inside of the buildings retain the feel of an elegant summer home in the mountains. The Fireside Room, the main wedding reception area, is large, with stone walls, beamed ceilings, and windows which overlook the grounds. With the adjoining large patio, this makes a nice spot for a wedding and reception. The Carriage Room is similar in décor, but smaller, and also opens out to a nice patio. Many wedding parties reserve the Gazebo for a small wedding or for pictures. With the mansion open to the public and the possibility of three weddings going on at once on the grounds, this is not the most private spot for a wedding, but you could book the entire mansion if this is your goal. Try days other than Saturdays, and try off-season for lower prices and a quieter wedding at this center.

BROOK FOREST INN/THE PINECONE ROOM
8136 Brook Forest Road
Evergreen, CO 80439
303-674-9919
Space available: Three rooms
Number of people: 100 in the main room; 250 with all three rooms
Price and services included: $200 for three hours; $25 each additional hour
Price includes rental of the rooms only.
Time available: Morning to midnight
Catering: Provided; ask for prices
Liquor: Open and cash bar
Multiple events: No
Special services: Located at an inn with a restaurant
Directions: You can reach the Brook Forest Inn from two directions. Take I-70 west from Denver and exit at Evergreen Parkway. Follow Evergreen Parkway until you get to Evergreen. Turn right on Highway 73 at the stoplight in Evergreen and go two miles to Brook Forest Road. Turn south on Brook Forest Road and go 5.1 miles to the inn on the left. Or, take Highway 285 to Conifer. From Conifer, take Highway 73 toward Evergreen to Brook Forest Road. Turn south on Brook Forest Road and go 5.1 miles to the inn.

Located in the historic Brook Forest Inn, the Pinecone Room is a light, airy room, with wood floors and walls, and a floor-to-ceiling quartz fireplace. For a sit-down dinner, this room, separated from the hotel by glass doors, is an ideal setting. Adjacent to it are the piano lounge and parlor room, which can be used as well and would be a good addition for cocktail receptions. Both these rooms are warm, elegant, and refined with European antiques, a baby grand piano, and a comfortable bar. Catering is provided at an additional charge by the inn's restaurant, and their food is usually excellent.

Courtesy of Chief Hosa

A complete wedding facility, Chief Hosa is a popular historic site in the foothills.

CHIEF HOSA LODGE

27661 Genesee Drive
Golden, CO 80401
303-526-0364

Space available: One great room with adjoining rooms and deck.

Number of people: 165 for a sit-down dinner; 200 for a cocktail reception; 250 for a cocktail reception with the outside patio.

Price and services included: $775 (Sunday-Friday); $1050 (Saturday); $175 (wedding ceremony-additional)

Price includes a five-hour rental, DJ, bartenders, wait staff, set-up/clean-up, tables, chairs, dishes, cake cutter, tea, coffee, silk flower centerpieces, candles, sound system, and CDs.

Time available: 12-5 p.m./6-11 p.m.

Catering: Provided. All buffets with unlimited trips; one menu item per party. Prices average about $17/person, depending on entrée. Entrées range from Italian dinners to prime rib.

Liquor: Bring your own. Beer, wine, and champagne only. Cash or open bar.

Multiple events: No

Special services: Everything is done for you; use of entire grounds, including pool and outdoor sports equipment; campground next door; wedding coordinator. Chief Hosa also does many corporate winter parties.

Directions: Take I-70 west from Denver to the Chief Hosa exit.

History lives in the walls of this lodge. Built in the early 1900s as part of the Denver Mountain Parks system, the lodge has served as a museum, gambling hall, bordello, restaurant, youth hostel, and finally wedding/celebrations facility. Stone walls, wood-beamed ceilings, fireplaces, and long wooden tables inside comprise the atmosphere of this lodge. The main room connects several smaller rooms, including an old stone chapel (perfect for a small wedding), and sitting room with comfortable couches and an inviting fireplace. Outside, the deck boasts grand views of the Continental Divide and is another nice site for the ceremony. You will need to supply a few essentials for your ceremony such as photographer and fresh flowers, but everything else is provided, and the staff at Chief Hosa is exceptional.

CRYSTAL ROSE/ROBIN'S NEST

636 Lookout Mountain Road
Golden, CO 80401
303-526-7530 (Crystal Rose or Robin's Nest)

Space available: One large room at each facility and outside yard or deck.

Number of people: Crystal Rose: 100-250 for a sit-down dinner (more with cocktail party); Robin's Nest: 150-max.

Price and services included: $35/person depending on choice of dinner-buffet or sit-down. Minimum number of people needed to reserve.
Price includes rental, tables, linens, china, glasses, fresh cut flowers, brass arch, candelabra, set-up and clean-up, DJ and food.

Time available: 8 a.m.-4 p.m./6 p.m.-2 a.m. Friday through Sunday.

Catering: Provided. Entrées range from hors' d'oeuvres, brunch, and buffets with roast beef or chicken teriyaki to sit-down dinners with prime rib, baked salmon, or chicken cordon bleu. Included with price.

Liquor: Cash bar provided.

Multiple events: No

Special services: They do everything. Theme parties available. Corporate parties a specialty. Volleyball pit and horseshoe pit available at Crystal Rose. Call to ask about corporate prices.
Directions: Take I-70 west from Denver to the Lookout Mountain exit. Follow the signs to Buffalo Bill's Memorial Museum and Grave. You'll see both these locations about 0.5 miles before you reach Buffalo Bill's Memorial Museum and Grave.

This is another place where a lot of the fine print is taken care of for you. Crystal Rose and Robin's Nest are part of a five-facility chain and are well-used throughout the year for weddings and corporate parties. Perched atop Lookout Mountain, both locations have the best views in the chain. The Crystal Rose is larger with windows that look out on city lights and an outside back yard where they hold weddings. The Robin's Nest is smaller and resembles a VFW from the front but has a nice view of a lake from the back windows and again has a pleasant yard for weddings. Both have fireplaces, dance floors, and full bars. A reader's poll in the *Rocky Mountain News* voted this chain one of the best places to throw a party.

THE DAILEY CABIN
4395 Independence Trail
Evergreen, CO 80439
303-674-3577; 1-800-459-2406
Space available: One room with smaller adjoining room
Number of people: 16 people for a sit-down dinner; 20 people for a cocktail party
Price and services included: $75/hour with three-hour minimum.
   Price includes room rental. Glassware and linens can be rented for an additional cost.
Time available: 8 a.m.-10 p.m. weekdays; 11 p.m. weekends
Catering: Hire own. Needs to be approved by Highland Haven.
Liquor: Open bar only. Caterers need license.
Multiple events: No
Special services: Inn is right there
Directions: Take I-70 west from Denver and exit at Evergreen Parkway. Follow Evergreen Parkway eight miles. You'll go through Evergreen to reach Independence Trail and the Highland Haven on the right.

Smaller than any other center, the Dailey Cabin is listed here because of its charm. Surviving as the oldest cabin in Evergreen, this place feels solid and has an old mountain feeling. Antiques, Persian rugs, and timber logs complete the décor of this small room which is attached to the Highland Haven Inn. If it's a small quiet gathering you are desiring with very convenient lodging for guests, this place might fit the ticket.

EL RANCHO VILLAGE
29260 Highway 40
Golden, CO 80401
303-526-0661
Space available: Two large rooms on bottom floor of El Rancho
Number of people: 100 people in each room downstairs
Price and services included: $300 for each room; $500 for both rooms
   Price includes rental only.
Time available: Five-hour blocks of time up to midnight
Catering: Provided. Average $23/person, depending on buffet or sit-down dinner. Choices ranging from trout, cowboy steak, and rack of lamb to veal. Hot or cold hors' d'oeuvres also available.
Liquor: Open or cash bar.
Multiple events: Yes
Special services: Wedding consultation with personalized style.
Directions: Take I-70 west from Denver to the Evergreen exit. You'll see El Rancho on the west or right side of the road off the exit.

   In addition to the restaurant, gift shop, and bar, El Rancho offers two places to hold celebrations. The two rooms are downstairs and a bit dark, but with patios leading outside. The rooms are connected by an open doorway, and it is possible to have two weddings at once separated only by a curtain. Pay for both rooms if this is a problem. El Rancho caters events held here. Catering manager Bryan enjoys helping couples plan their wedding, and so a wedding here is fairly stress-free.

EVERGREEN CONFERENCE CENTER
27618 Fireweed Drive
Evergreen, CO 80437
303-674-3525
Space available: Two connecting rooms rented as one
Number of people: 160-max using the decks. 100-130 for a sit-down dinner.
Price and services included: $500 for four hours; $100 for each additional hour
   Price includes room rental, chairs, tables, dishes, glasses, tablecloths, flatware, set-up, and clean-up.
Time available: Four-hour time blocks. Finished by 11 p.m.
Catering: Hire own from approved list.
Liquor: Bring your own. Can't sell alcohol.
Multiple events: No
Special services: Six-bedroom lodge available next door. $55/room with two beds. Center has a list of various wedding providers.

Directions: Take I-70 west to the Evergreen exit and follow Evergreen Parkway past Safeway to the turn for Hiwan Homestead Museum. Take this road past the Hiwan Homestead Museum until you get to Iris Drive (near the 7-11). Follow Iris Drive all the way until it ends at Fireweed Lane. Evergreen Conference Center is on your right.

Located close to Main Street Evergreen, the Evergreen Conference Center was first built as a spiritual retreat center for the Episcopal church which sits across the street. Both rooms in the historic building are light and airy, and a wooden deck opens up the dining room to nice views of the evergreen trees. The parlor room, with its hardwood floors and brick fireplace, would serve well as a site for a ceremony. Although events need to be finished by 11 p.m., for an additional price, guests can retire to the center's lodge next door where a comfortable gathering room with refrigerator, microwave, coffee maker, and VCR available. The lodge can sleep 12 people and is clean, simple, and convenient.

EVERGREEN ELKS LODGE
27972 Iris Drive, P.O. Box 298
Evergreen, CO 80439
303-674-5591
Space available: One large room, smaller room, patio
Number of people: 300 for a sit-down dinner in the large room; 80 on the patio; 60 in the smaller room
Price and services included: Large room: $700; Smaller room or patio: $250; Kitchen use: $75
Price includes rental of the facility for unlimited hours, tables, chairs
Time available: Any time, except when Elks functions are scheduled; can go until 2 a.m.
Catering: Hire own.
Liquor: Liquor provided for charge; can't bring own liquor.
Multiple events: No
Directions: Take I-70 west to the Evergreen exit and follow Evergreen Parkway past Safeway to the turn for Hiwan Homestead Museum. Take this road past the Hiwan Homestead Museum until you get to Iris Drive (near the 7-11). Turn left on Iris. The Elks Lodge is on Iris Drive, shortly after you make the turn.

For large parties at an inexpensive price, the Elks Lodge in Evergreen is great. Inside this large building, just east of Main Street Evergreen, is a casual ballroom where many celebrations are held. There's a 1600-square-foot dance floor and two rooms which can open into one to provide the maximum seating. The patio outside is a small fenced backyard with covered tables and barbecue grills. Celebrations can continue until 2 a.m. if needed, and the Elks seem pretty flexible.

Lori Hladik

In the center of Evergreen, the Evergreen Lake House hosts many beautiful weddings.

EVERGREEN LAKE HOUSE
29614 Upper Bear Creek Road
P.O. Box 520
Evergreen, CO 80437
303-674-0532
Space available: Two rooms
Number of people: 150 in the Great Room; 40 in the Octagon Room. Most parties rent both.
Price and services included: Great Room: $275/hour; both rooms: $350/hour
   Price includes room rental of the facility, chairs, and tables.
Time available: April 1 through mid-November only. Minimal rental is two hours; celebrations must finish by midnight.
Catering: Hire own.
Liquor: Bring your own with prior approval. Can't sell alcohol.
Multiple events: No.
Special services: Lake House staff sets up chairs and tables.
Directions: Take I-70 west from Denver and get off at the Evergreen exit. Follow Evergreen Parkway into the heart of Evergreen. You'll see the lake on the southwest side of the road. You can't miss it.

A popular spot, the Evergreen Lake House is the center to use for a beautiful mid-sized wedding. Home to Evergreen's outdoor ice skating in the winter, the Lake House is only available for celebrations in the spring, summer, and fall months. The Great Room has wood floors, log walls, a stone fireplace, and windows on three sides that overlook the lake and surrounding hills. Adjoining this room is the smaller Octagon Room with additional fantastic views of the lake. Guests can also use the outside decks and walk down to the lake. Drawbacks to the Lake House include its price, strict rules, and minimal kitchen facilities. However, if not on a limited budget, the benefits of this impressive lodge in the center of Evergreen outweigh the few drawbacks.

MOUNT VERNON COUNTRY CLUB
24933 Clubhouse Circle
Golden, CO 80401
303-526-3105
Space available: Five rooms
Number of people: 350 for a sit-down dinner in the main dining room; 200 for a sit-down dinner in the Canyon-Trail Room (can be split into two rooms); 120 for a sit-down dinner in the Aspen Room; 90 for a sit-down dinner in the lounge; 32 for a sit-down dinner in the board room.
Price and services included: $400-850; $150 in the board room
   Price includes room rental. Catering charge includes the rest of the services-set-up, clean-up, tables, chairs, and linens.
Time available: 8 a.m.-3:30 p.m./5:30-midnight. The lounge is only open Saturday from 8 a.m.-3:30 p.m.
Catering: Provided. Additional charge. Buffets: $15-23; sit-down dinners $17-24. Entrées range from vegetarian feasts to prime rib, veal, king crab, and stuffed shrimp. Many choices available.
Liquor: Cash or open bar.
Multiple events: Yes
Special services: They provide everything, including planning. Member prices are substantially less. Corporate parties and meetings.
Directions: Take I-70 west from Denver to the Lookout Mountain exit. Take this exit and head straight ahead or due north on Country Club Road until you reach Mt. Vernon Road. Go right or east until you get to the club which is on your left.

When it comes to classy places, Mt. Vernon Country Club is one of them. Built 75 years ago, the club resembles a renovated old hotel. With a number of different rooms to hold weddings and a vast selection of good food to choose from, this facility has something for everyone. The main dining room at this club is the largest room around to hold celebrations. Many weddings take place on the decks,

Courtesy of Mount Vernon Country Club

Mount Vernon Country Club is a classy large facility with sweeping views.

which have great views of the mountains and city lights, and then the wedding party has reserved a room inside for the reception. Inside, the various rooms are light with a lot of windows and tastefully decorated. Although five different weddings could take place at once, the rooms are far enough apart in this large club so you wouldn't hear or see other wedding parties. Everything needs to be provided by Mount Vernon Country Club, and what they offer is first-class.

THE PINES AT GENESEE
633 Park Point Drive
Golden, CO 80401
303-526-7939
Space available: Two levels; four break-out rooms for conferences
Number of people: Upper level: 200 sit-down; 300 buffet. Lower level: 100 sit-down; 150 buffet
Price and services included: $1,500-$1800
Price includes room rental, tables, chairs, event planning, china, flatware, bridal changing rooms and dance floors.
Time available: 9 a.m.-4 p.m./5 p.m.-midnight Friday-Sunday

Catering: Provided by LeBrian's Gourmet Catering. Additional charge. $18-26. Eclectic walk-around-feasts to buffet dinners with cuisine such as Bourbon Grilled Cornish Hen, Mesquite Salmon and Lobster Quesadillas.
Liquor: Bring your own.
Multiple events: Yes
Special services: Personalized event planning. Corporate meetings.
Directions: Take I-70 to the Genesee/Lookout Mountain exit and turn left or south toward Genesee. Go left at Genesee Trail Road and take the second right onto Park Point Drive. Follow Park Point to the traffic circle, and you'll see The Pines just east of the building with the green dome.

Open since May 1997, this facility offers Front Range residents another large place to hold weddings. Rooms are carpeted, air-conditioned and fairly separate from one another. The upper level is much sunnier, larger, and more expensive. Downstairs has a nice fireplace with an outside patio that overlooks the city. Resembling a new hotel, this facility is modern and conveniently close to Denver. Again, a lot of on-site planning is taken care of for you, including the catering which offers some of the most diverse ethnic cuisine around.

WILLOW RIDGE
4903 Willow Spring Road
Morrison, CO 80465
303-697-6951
Space available: One large room, adjoining parlor, living room and upstairs rooms
Number of people: 100 for a sit-down dinner; 200 for a buffet, using the decks
Price and services included: $875-1100 depending on number of people and time; $150 extra for ceremony.
Price includes rental of the facility, tables, and chairs.
Time available: 11 a.m.-5 p.m./6 p.m.-midnight
Catering: Hire own. Must be licensed
Liquor: Bring your own. Can't sell liquor.
Multiple events: No
Special services: Manager has recommendations for service providers.
Directions: Take Highway 285 south from Denver to the Morrison exit. Willow Ridge is the large white building just off the highway before you reach The Fort restaurant.

This white southern-style mansion, dating back to the turn of the century, overlooks the city and the red rocks of Morrison. Elegant and formal, the mansion offers a main ballroom with deck for celebrations, along with a parlor, living room, wet bar, and upstairs rooms. The entire facility is rented at once, so there is plenty of room for guests to mingle.   Not as in-house as many of the centers, the couple will need to take care of a lot of the details.   However, for an attractive and different celebration facility, Willow Ridge is worth checking out.

K. Blum

An elegant southern mansion in the foothills, Willow Ridge is another beautiful wedding center choice.

Chapter Eight
Practical Information

Note: *Calling from Bailey, Conifer, and Pine to the Denver metropolitan area is often long-distance. Check the local phone book for information.*

AMBULANCE, FIRE, POLICE

For any serious emergency, call 911. Other important numbers follow. Remember in certain areas you may need to dial 1+ area code (303) + listed number.

Colorado State Patrol (non-injury road accidents):	303-239-4501
TTY:	303-239-4505
Jefferson County Sheriff:	303-277-0211
Morrison Police Department (Morrison only):	303-697-4810
Park County Sheriff (Bailey):	303-838-4441
Poison Control—local:	303-739-1123
—Outside Denver metro area:	1-800-332-3073
TTY:	303-739-1127

For administrative concerns, the following are numbers of the local fire and rescue squads in the area. All are volunteer organizations.

Elk Creek Fire Department:	303-674-5770 or 303-838-5575
Evergreen Fire Department:	303-674-3145
Indian Hills Fire Department	303-697-4568
Lookout Mountain Fire Protection District:	303-526-0707
Platte Canyon Fire and Rescue:	303-838-5853

BANKS

Following are banks in the area. All are linked to 24-hour instant cash machines which accept cards bearing the Cirrus or Plus symbols and generally Mastercard or Visa.

BERGEN PARK
First Bank (King Soopers Complex; 303-679-9900)

CONIFER
Colorado Community First (26291 Main Street; 303-674-0649)
Peak National Bank (26699 Pleasant Park Road; 303-838-3070)

EVERGREEN
Colorado Community First (3779 Evergreen Parkway; 303-674-6646)
Colorado National Bank (2922 Highway 74; 303-674-0264)
  An ATM for this bank can also be found at the 7-11 (27883 Meadow Drive).
Evergreen National Bank (Main Street; 303-674-2700)
First Bank (30770 Stagecoach Boulevard; 303-679-1000)
Peak National Bank (1248 Evergreen Parkway; 303-670-3200)

CALENDAR OF EVENTS

Following is a list of events happening throughout the mountain communities. Check with the number provided or consult one of the local newspapers for more information.

JANUARY
Check your local newspaper.

FEBRUARY
Ragtime Bash
  Ragtime musicians from around the United States gather to perform and educate. Evergreen Elks Lodge 303-674-5591. Cost.

MARCH
Easter Egg Hunt
  Thousands of eggs for the finding. Conifer 303-838-0178. Free.

APRIL
Handbell Concert
Handbell concert by the Mountain Ringers. Evergreen Lake House. 303-674-2460 or 303-674-0378. Free.

MAY
Check your local newspaper.

JUNE
Evergreen Rodeo
Celebrating over 30 years, the Evergreen Rodeo, with parade, dances, barbecue, and rodeo, is one of the larger events in the area. Evergreen. 303-670-3928. Parade is free. Other events cost.
Garden Market
Plants, flowers from local gardens for sale. 303-674-0496. Cost.
National Repertory Orchestra Concert
Alderfer/Three Sisters Open Space Park, Evergreen. 303-674-1190. Cost.
Rhubarb Festival
Taste, smell, and see luscious rhubarb at this annual event. Pine. 303-838-4373. Free.
Rocky Mountain Indian Festival
Native American culture, art, performances. Heritage Grove, Evergreen. 303-674-6262. Free.

JULY
5K Freedom Run
Run to benefit Mt. Evans Hospice. Evergreen. 303-674-6400. Cost.
Conifer Art Fair
Over 50 booths by local and Colorado artisans. Excellent artwork. West Jefferson Elementary School, Conifer. Free.
Evergreen Garden Club's Garden Tour
Tour of mountain home gardens. Evergreen 303-674-0496. Happens every other year (July 99, next tour). Cost.
Evergreen Town Celebration
Trout Unlimited's fishing clinic for kids, concerts, food. Evergreen Lake, Evergreen. 303-674-1190 or 303-674-6745. Free.
Indian Hills 4th of July Celebration
Pancake breakfast, community garage sale to benefit next year's fireworks, parade, community potluck, fireworks at dusk! Fireworks are the best around. Arrive early. Indian Hills. 303-697-4568. Most events (including fireworks) free. Donations accepted.

Summerfest Arts and Crafts Fair
Over 100 artisans. Heritage Grove Park, Evergreen. 303-674-4625. Free.

Triple ByPass Bike Race
Sponsored by Team Evergreen, this tough but rewarding bike race runs through the area. 303-674-6048. Cost.

AUGUST

Bailey Day
Booths, entertainment, rides, Five-Mile Mountain Run, Black Powder Shoot, and town fun. Bailey. 303-838-4343. Free.

Doggie Olympics
Mazes, obstacle courses, and even a cake walk for dogs and the entire family. Heritage Grove Park, Evergreen. 303-674-8711. Cost.

Evergreen Town Race
10K and 5K run along Upper Bear Creek Road to benefit the Alpine Rescue Team. Evergreen. 303-674-0532. Cost.

Evergreen Arts Festival
Over 30 years in Evergreen. Artists from all over the United States. Similar in caliber to Cherry Creek Arts Festival. Heritage Grove Park, Evergreen. 303-674-6262. Free.

Fireman's Fair
Two-day event honors local volunteer firemen.   Games, booths, Fireman Olympics. Conifer. 303-838-0178. Cost.

Mountain Music Festival
Nine bands, food, drink, activities. Evergreen Lake, Evergreen. 303-674-0532. Cost.

SEPTEMBER

Morrison Cowboy Celebration
Cowboy poetry, arts and crafts. Morrison. 303-697-8749. Some events cost.

Tie-Dye Festival
Bands, activities, food, tie-dye tent, drumming after dark. Evergreen Lake, Evergreen. 303-674-5843. Cost.

OCTOBER

Bluegrass Festival
Live bands, food, all-day. Evergreen Elks Lodge, Evergreen. 303-674-5591. Cost.

Cider Days
Bring your own apples and have them pressed into cider with an old-fashioned cider press. Bear Creek Nursing Center, Morrison. 303-697-8181. Free.

K. Blum

The Evergreen Arts Festival brings artists from all over the country.

Evening of the Arts

Fine art, music, nationally known musicians perform to benefit scholarships and loans for Evergreen area high school graduates. Evergreen Lake House, Evergreen. 303-674-7199 or 303-670-0438. Cost.

Halloween Celebration

Games, candy, activities, very scary haunted house. Evergreen. 303-674-0532. Some events cost.

Pumpkin Giveaway

Free pumpkins, cider, food. Come by 9 a.m.! Moore & Company Realty, Aspen Park. 303-674-0575. Free.

Safe Halloween

Merchants provide kids with candy and a safe place to get their treats. Conifer. 303-838-0178. Free.

NOVEMBER

Conifer Newcomers and Neighbors Holiday Boutique
Arts and crafts galore; good chance to purchase Christmas items. Conifer. 303-838-0178. Free.

Turkey Shopping Walk
Walk through Adobe Creek Artist Center's Galleries Evening. Adobe Creek Artists Center, Kittredge. 303-674-4109. Free.

DECEMBER

bRing in the Holidays
Handbell festival. Handbell choirs from around Colorado. Conifer High School, Conifer. 303-674-2460 or 303-674-0378. Free.

Christmas Celebration
Breakfast with Santa, tree lighting. Evergreen. 303-674-3412. Free.

Conifer Christmas Parade
Local parade with everyone involved. Twelve days of Christmas—all shops with sales. Conifer. 303-838-0178. Free.

Holiday Walk
Downtown businesses open late, music, activities. Heritage Grove and Main Street, Evergreen. 303-674-6262. Free.

Morrison Town Christmas
Downtown Morrison. 303-697-8749. Free.

Skate the Lake
New Year's Eve celebration at the Evergreen Lake with activities and skating for children and adults. Evergreen Lake House, Evergreen. 303-674-6441. Cost.

Winterfest
100+ arts and crafts exhibits and entertainment. Evergreen Middle School, Evergreen. 303-674-4625. Cost.

CHAMBERS OF COMMERCE

The **Evergreen Area Chamber of Commerce** (29029 Upper Bear Creek Road/Lakepoint Center, Evergreen, CO; 303-674-3412) is chock-full of information on the foothills area and has newcomer packages available. **Conifer's Chamber of Commerce** (Safeway Center, Conifer, CO; 303-838-0178) is open in the Pack N Mail Office six days/week and offers information on Conifer and the Highway 285 corridor. If you have further questions, Sue Wilson, who staffs this office part-time, has great information. The **Platte Canyon Chamber of Commerce** (Bailey, CO; 303-838-9080) can give you more information on Park County.

CHILD CARE

There are many options for child care. Included is a sampling from the different mountain communities. For further guidance, contact one of the chambers of commerce, the phone book, churches, or local schools.

Child Garden Learning Center (27071 Barkley Road, Conifer, CO; 303-838-2627)
Children's World Learning Center (1035 El Rancho Road, Evergreen, CO; 303-526-4160)
Early Learning Center (19423 N. Turkey Creek, Morrison, CO; 303-697-9595)
Elk Creek Child Development Center (13224 Highway 285, Pine, CO; 303-838-7182)
Montessori School of Conifer (25782 Vosler Street, Aspen Park; 303-674-2544)
Panther's Perch (4460 Parmalee Gulch, Indian Hills, CO; 303-697-4252)
Only the Best Nannies (303-670-7738)
Our House Children's Learning Center (6891 Highway 73, Marshdale, CO; 303-674-3684)

CLIMATE

Enviable is the word that describes the climate here. At elevations higher than the mile-high city in a state where sunshine is the norm, the mountain communities seem to be pleasant year-round. The weather here is generally a bit cooler than in Denver. In the summer, this means relief from hot arid days, and in the winter, this means more opportunity for skiing, skating, sledding, and numerous other winter activities.

Summertime temperatures range from high 70s to low 80s and sometimes drop down to cool upper 50s at night. During the afternoon, the skies often cloud over and refresh the area with showers. It usually doesn't last more than an hour or two, and afterwards, the sun is out again and the sky clear. For the evenings, you'll probably want a light jacket or sweater.

Winter averages 90 inches of snowfall a year, and temperatures range from the 40s down to five degrees. Snow is light and powdery and usually doesn't create too many problems on mountain roads. Front-wheel drive and studded snow tires help make life easier in the wintertime and are usually adequate. Remember that four-wheel drive vehicles don't help much on ice.

Fall is glorious with temperatures in the 60s to the 70s and the aspen trees and elk putting on their show. Spring hovers in the 60s and warms up slowly. Overall, the area gets many days of sunshine; in fact, almost every day the sun comes out. It's hard to beat! To really read up on climate, check out the Colorado Climate Center's website: ulysses.atmos.colostate.edu.

FIRE SAFETY

This listing gives you a few practical tips on preventing forest fires while in the wilderness whether you are playing or living here. This is a major concern for area residents. In March of 1991, 55 acres burned in nearby O'Fallon Park; Buffalo Creek is still recovering from their devastating fire in 1996 where 11,875 acres and many homes burned. An area around Mt. Evans recently became the victim of a tossed cigarette or unattended campfire. Every year there are fires in the Front Range, and with increased growth, there is likely to be more damage to property and many lives lost. In order to manage the forests, the United States Forest Service does prescribe fires several times a year in certain areas. These fires are controlled and enhance the ecosystem and wildlife habitat. In addition, they help minimize the chance of a devastating wildfire later on. There are things you can do to help as well.

WHEN CAMPING

Avoid encircling the campfire with rocks. Rocks may explode with intense heat.
Build campfires away from overhanging branches, steep slopes, rotten stumps, logs, dry grass, and leaves.
Keep water and a shovel handy.
Keep campfires small.
Make sure no tree roots are burning and that the fire is cool before you sleep at night.
Never leave a campfire unattended.
When finished, drown the fire with water; stir what remains and drown again.

AT HOME

Burn safely when burning debris (You'll usually need a permit).
Clean your roof.
Control vegetation. (Establish a fuel break at least 30 feet wide around structures.)

Develop a water supply.
Install a spark arrester on your chimney.
Keep your chimney clean.
Plan adequate access and escape (wide driveways and grades lower than 12%).
Have fire tools handy.
Store firewood away from your home.
Use only approved wood burning devices.
Use fire resistant building material.

You can call the **Colorado State Forest Service's Small Acreage Management Program** (303-279-9757) to get information about how to protect your home from fire hazards. They will also inspect your property for wildfire risks for $65, a small fee to pay when you consider the potential consequences of fire. In addition, you can call **Jefferson County Emergency Preparedness** (303-271-8215) to find out more information.

GOVERNMENT

Except for Morrison and Bailey, most of the area is unincorporated Jefferson and Park County and is governed by the county. There is talk of incorporating Evergreen and Conifer, yet, the issue remains stalled. Every four years commissioners are elected. John Stone, Patricia Holloway, and Michelle Lawrence are the current Jefferson County Commissioners. To contact them, call 303-271-8525 or write to them at the Jefferson County Building, 100 Jefferson County Parkway, Golden, CO 80419.

Bailey is a part of unincorporated Park County, and it likewise has three commissioners. Robert Barford, C.J. DeLang, and Lynda James are the current Park County commissioners. To contact them, call 303-980-1836 extension 201, or write them at P.O. Box 220, Fairplay, CO 80440.

Since 1906, Morrison has been an incorporated town and is run by a board of seven trustees, including a mayor. Every four years trustees are elected, and they hold public meetings the first and third Tuesdays of the month at 7:30 p.m. at Town Hall in Morrison. To find out more information on Morrison's government, attend one of the meetings, phone 303-697-8749, or visit their web page: town.morrison.co.us.

LATE NIGHT SERVICES

Most of the large supermarkets are open 24 hours. **Albertsons** (30931 Stagecoach Boulevard, Evergreen, CO; 303-679-0403) is the exception, and it opens at 5 a.m. and closes at 1 a.m. There are several gas stations open 24 hours, and those are also listed.

Loaf 'N Jug
   9904 Highway 285, Conifer, CO; 303-838-6684
7-11
   27883 Meadow Drive, Evergreen, CO; 303-670-0090
King Soopers
   1173 Highway 74, Bergen Park, CO; 303-674-8249
Safeway
   Highway 285 & 73, Conifer, CO; 303-838-9868
Safeway
   High Country Square/Highway 74, Evergreen, CO; 303-674-6625

MAGAZINES AND NEWSPAPERS

CANYON COURIER
303-674-5534
   The area's major newspaper, it is published weekly and circulates throughout the foothills area.

CITY AND MOUNTAIN VIEWS
303-526-2420
   This news-magazine covers the I-70 corridor and is available six times a year.

COLORADO SERENITY
303-670-5448
   A local magazine published monthly, *Colorado Serenity* focuses on people and lifestyles in the foothills.

THE DENVER POST
303-832-3232
   One of Colorado's two major newspapers, it circulates throughout this region.

HIGH TIMBER TIMES
303-838-4884
   Another major newspaper in the foothills area, this one primarily covers the Highway 285 corridor and is published weekly.

JEFFERSON, THE COUNTY MAGAZINE
303-279-5541

This magazine profiles Jefferson County with many highlights of the entire county, including the foothills.

MOUNTAIN CONNECTION
303-763-6316
Published monthly, this newspaper is distributed throughout Conifer and the Highway 285 corridor and brings area residents good news only. They are also online: mtnconnection.com

ROCKY MOUNTAIN NEWS
303-892-6397
Colorado's other major newspaper, available throughout the area.

MEDICAL SERVICES

There are no hospitals in the area, but there are several urgent care facilities. The closest hospital for most residents is **Lutheran Medical Center** (8300 W. 38th Avenue, Wheat Ridge, CO; 303-425-4500). Most urgent care centers listed below are open late and take walk-ins. Check hours first.

CONIFER
Conifer Medical Center
26659 Pleasant Park Road; 303-674-0605
Open Monday-Friday: 8 a.m.-9 p.m.; Saturday: 8 a.m.-8 p.m.; Sunday: 9 a.m.-5 p.m.

Conifer Mountain Family Medicine
10791 Kitty Drive, next to Conifer Safeway; 303-838-4686 or 303-674-7875
Open Monday-Wednesday: 7 a.m.-7 p.m.; Tuesday-Thursday: 8.am.-7 p.m.; Friday: 8 a.m.-5 p.m.; Saturday: 8 a.m.-12 p.m.. Doctor on call.

Mt. Evans Hospice

Since 1980, the Mt. Evans Hospice & Home Health Care has provided care to sick, disabled, or terminally ill patients in their own homes. This non-profit agency offers various support groups and programs. They provide the following invaluable services to the communities:

Certified home health aides
Medical social workers
Nondenominational chaplains
Physical, occupational, and speech therapists
Registered dieticians
Registered nurses on call 24 hours/day
Skilled nursing care
Trained respite volunteers

3721 Evergreen Parkway, Suite 9; 303-674-6400.

EVERGREEN/BERGEN PARK

Bergen Park Health Center
1520 Evergreen Parkway/Highway 74; 303-670-1616
  Open Monday-Friday: 8 a.m.-9 p.m.; Saturday-Sunday: 9 a.m.-5 p.m..
  Connected with "Ask-A-Nurse" by calling the office after hours.

Mountain Family Medicine
30810 Stage Coach Boulevard, Suite 101; 303-674-3370
  Open Monday-Friday: 7:30 a.m.-6:30 p.m.; Saturday: 9 a.m.-5 p.m.;
  Sunday: closed. Doctor is available through answering service after
  hours.

ORGANIZATIONS/SUPPORT GROUPS

No matter where your tastes lie, there is sure to be an organization or
club that meets your needs. Some are detailed here. Most are listed.
New ones are forming all the time. For numbers and information on
groups, contact the local chamber of commerce or local churches.

Lora Abcarian, Shadow Catcher Photography

The face of community service, the Conifer Kiwanis Club.

ORGANIZATIONS

4-H Club (719-836-4289)
285 Sertoma (303-838-4703)
American Association of University Women (303-674-4491)
American Association of Retired Persons (303-838-4258)
Bear Creek Rodeo Association (303-674-5365 or 303-670-3928)
Bloodhound Investigators (303-674-8317)
  This group provides trained bloodhound assistance to search and res-
  cue groups, law enforcement, and the public, both locally and nation-
  ally. In addition, they provide information on bloodhounds' care,
  maintenance, training, and adoption.
Boy Scouts (303-674-7308 or 303-674-4091)
Blue Spruce Kiwanis (303-674-7853)
BPOE (Elks) (303-674-5591)
Conifer Kiwanis (303-838-0178)
Conifer Lions (303-838-7233)
Conifer Newcomers Club (303-838-0178)
Daughters of the American Revolution (303-670-3572)
Drive Smart (303-674-0789)
Ducks Unlimited (303-674-3892)
Evergreen Animal Protective League (303-674-6442)
Evergreen Area Council for the Arts (303-674-4625)
  A private, non-profit board who promotes and encourages all aspects
  of the arts in the mountain community. The EACA works as an
  umbrella organization, especially for start-up arts groups and arts
  organizations who want to take their organization to another level. Its
  main functions are sponsorship of two large art fairs each year:
  Summerfest in July and Winterfest in December (see Calendar of
  Events). In addition, it makes grants to area art groups and serves the
  Arts in the Schools program.
Evergreen Artists Association (303-674-1620)
  A private, non-profit group dedicated to furthering artists and the arts.
  They hold monthly meetings where artists demonstrate their skills as
  well as hold two member shows throughout the year. The August Fine
  Arts Fair, held in Evergreen, is their main event (see "Calendar of
  Events").
Evergreen Garden Club (303-674-5965)
  A well-established Evergreen club, this non-profit organization holds
  monthly meetings with speakers on mountain gardening topics, tends
  six community gardens in the foothills area, and goes on field trips to
  various gardens and centers.
Evergreen Kiwanis Club (303-674-6667)

Evergreen Naturalists Audobon Society (303-674-6580)

With monthly meetings, Saturday hikes and walks, educational programs, plus wildflower, birds, and star gazing trips, this organization always has something going on for the nature lover. In addition, the Evergreen chapter participates in the nationwide Christmas bird count and tracks birds in the local area.

Evergreen Newcomers (303-670-0587)

In existence for over 25 years, the Newcomers have been welcoming families to the foothills area and keeping them involved. The organization hosts a plethora of clubs from book groups and four-wheeling to skiing and wine tasting. Because of its fantastic range of activities, many "newcomers" have been involved in the activities for years.

Evergreen Senior Citizens Club (303-674-1894)

Evergreen Women's Club (303-674-5667)

Over 50 years old, this is the longest standing club in the area. They hold numerous activities and meetings throughout the year.

Farmers Union (303-838-5215)

Friendship Bridge (303-674-0717)

Girl Scouts (Bailey) (303-838-5799)

Girl Scouts (Clear Creek) (303-670-7704)

Girl Scouts (Jefferson) (303-674-6917)

Golden K Kiwanis of Shadow Mountain, Conifer (303-838-9066)

Habit for Humanity, Blue Spruce (303-674-1127)

The foothills' branch of this nationally-known organization gives low-income mountain families the opportunity to own their own homes. Volunteers work with the families in the construction and various other aspects of home ownership.

Intermountain Humane Society (303-838-2668)

League of Women Voters (303-238-0032)

Mountain Area Democrats (303-674-1421)

Mountain Area Home-Based Business Network (303-838-2960)

Mountain Area Recycling Group (303-670-3711)

Mountain Doers Craft Club (303-838-5662)

Mountain Family Resource Center (303-838-7552)

For anything related to the family, from child care information to crisis help, this center provides it. By calling them, you have access to the different resources available in the community.

Mountain Greens (303-526-2332)

Mountain Mentoring Project (303-674-4089) Big Brother/Big Sister project in Evergreen.

Mountain Services, Senior Resource Center (303-674-2843 or 303-838-6075)

The largest seniors' resource center in the area for mountain residents provides weekly activities, educational programs, and Friday luncheons, among other services. They also offer transportation, legal aid, employment and volunteer opportunities, and various care programs.

Mountain Toastmasters (303-674-7238)
Mountain Weavers Guild (303-674-0632)
National Organization for Women (303-670-1661)
Optimist Club (303-670-3072)
Park County Democratic Party (303-838-9742)
Park County Republican Party (303-838-2390)
People Comforters (Minnie: 303-674-4013 or Mary: 303-697-9412)
Over 400 quilts a year are made by this group and given to the Jefferson County Sheriff where they are distributed to victims of tragedies and/or domestic abuse.
Rotary Club of Evergreen (303-674-4362)
Salvation Army (303-861-4833)
Sierra Club (303-838-2143 or 303-674-3149)
Trout Unlimited (303-674-1017)
Protecting rivers and educating people on how to use and sustain river environments is part of the mission of this well-established group. The group maintains local rivers, works with Jefferson County's Outdoor Lab School, and holds monthly meetings with nationally recognized speakers on fishing and river conservation.
Veterans of Foreign Wars (303-674-6598; 303-838-4343)
Wild Again Wildlife Rehabilitation (303-670-3309)
Youth Net Work (303-674-7422)
A nonprofit organization with a spiritual bent, sponsors breakfast and lunch clubs for teenagers and a weekly discipleship group.

SUPPORT GROUPS

Adult Grief Support Group (303-674-6400)
Adult Survivors of Incest Anonymous (303-674-6080)
Al-Anon (303-670-0622 and 303-838-5207)
Alcoholics Anonymous (303-322-4440)
Alzheimer's Support (303-674-5404)
Battered Women (303-838-7552)
Bereavement Support (303-674-4179)
Breast Cancer (303-278-2600)
Cancer Support (303-674-6400)
Caregivers Support (303-674-6400)
Children with Attention Deficit Disorder (303-674-0807)
Children's and Adolescents' Grief Support Group (303-674-6400)
Co-dependents Anonymous (303-838-2495)

Diabetic Support (303-670-1571)
La Leche League (303-697-3080 or 303-838-0315)
Lupus Support Group (303-832-2131)
Mothers of Pre-Schoolers (303-674-1089)
Multiple Sclerosis Support Group (303-674-6400)
Narcotics Anonymous (303-832-3784)
Neurofibromatosis (303-460-8313)
Parents/Friends of Lesbians & Gays (303-674-4843; 719-836-2456)
Parents' Grief Support Group (303-674-6400)
Parkinson's Disease Support (303-674-4325)
Spouses' Grief Support Group (303-674-6400)
Take Charge of Your Life (303-674-2843)
Take Pounds Off Sensibly (TOPS) (303-233-5888)
The following are addresses of local post offices in the area. Generally, post offices are open during the week from 8 a.m. to 5 p.m. and on Saturday from 8 a.m. to noon. But some hours do vary. Call 1-800-275-8777 for more information on any of the post offices.

POST OFFICES

Bailey Post Office (24 River Road, Bailey, CO; 80421)
Conifer (9546 S. Dallman Road, Conifer, CO; 80433)
Evergreen (3649 Highway 74, Evergreen, CO; 80439)
Indian Hills (5491 S. Parmalee Gulch Road, Indian Hills, CO; 80454)
Kittredge (26300 Hilltop Drive, Kittredge, CO; 80457)
Morrison (151 Summer Street, Morrison, CO; 80465)
Pine (187 Mt. Evans Boulevard, Pine, CO; 80470)

REAL ESTATE

Real estate in this area is hot. New homes are under construction throughout the region, older homes are at a premium, and prices are high. As of this writing, it's a sellers' market. In 1997, home prices increased by $20,000, making the average price of a home in Evergreen around $238,000. Since 1990, the average price of a home has skyrocketed over $100,000.

Realtors can be found in the phone book or through the **Evergreen-Conifer Association of Realtors,** an association which serves 500 real estate members. (29005 Upper Bear Creek Road, Evergreen, CO; 303-674-7020).

RECYCLING

There are many recycling spots, and some garbage collection companies offer recycling in the mountains. A handy pamphlet to recycling resources is "Recycling in the Mountains," published cooperatively by the Mt. Evans Sierra Club, Evergreen Naturalists Audobon Society, Evergreen Parks and Recreation, and Earth Day and Beyond. For any kind of hazardous waste (most everything marked "flammable," "Use with Caution," "Keep Away from Children"), take it to the **Jefferson County Household Chemical Collection Center** (151 S. Rooney Road, Golden, CO; 303-584-4646). For used tires, a company called **Jaitire** in Denver accepts them for a $1 fee. They grind them, and the pulp is used on athletic fields, equestrian areas, and playgrounds. Call 303-322-7887 for more information. For recycling home and office products, see the following:

EVERGREEN DISPOSAL
5801 Highway 73, Evergreen; 303-674-4147
Recycles aluminum and tin cans, plastic bottles #1 and #2, and newspapers, car batteries, glass containers, and scrap metal.

KING SOOPERS
Highway 74, Bergen Park, CO; 303-674-8249
One of the largest drop-off centers. They take aluminum cans, glass bottles, plastic grocery bags, foam meat trays and egg cartons, steel cans, newspapers, and plastic bottles #1 and #2.

SAFEWAY
25687 Highway 73, Conifer, CO; 303-838-9868
Recycles aluminum cans, plastic bottles #1 and #2, and newspaper.

WILL O'WISP
66666 Highway 285, Pine, CO; 303-838-2155
Aluminum and tin cans, plastic bottles #1 and #2, and newspapers, office paper, magazines, and slick paper.

RELIGIOUS ORGANIZATIONS

At last count there were 55 churches in the greater Evergreen area ranging from Charismatic to Catholic to New Age. For listings, consult the phone book or one of the chambers of commerce.

SCHOOLS

Public schools in the area are either in the Jefferson County School District or in the Platte Canyon District. Both school districts offer quality education. The Platte Canyon District runs from Kenosha Pass to the Jefferson County line in Pine Junction. Jefferson County includes communities from Pine Junction down to Morrison. For **Jefferson County**, call 303-982-6808. For **Platte Canyon**, call 303-838-7666.

The Outdoor Education Lab (303-674-3633) is a great resource for Jefferson County residents. Both the Outdoor Lab and its sister school, Windy Peak, offer all Jefferson County sixth graders the opportunity to spend a week in the mountains studying environmental and ecological issues, as well as doing activities like fly fishing and arts and crafts.

In addition to public schools, there are numerous private schools. To find out more about schooling options, consult one of the chambers of commerce.

WILDLIFE

K. Blum

Elk graze the hillsides of the foothills, and in fall, you can hear their bugling for miles around.

If you are living in the foothills, you are living in the natural habitat of a number of animals, including black bear, coyote, mountain lion, elk, deer, and smaller mammals like raccoons and squirrels. In the higher elevations, you will find mountain goats and bighorn sheep. Bears have made Colorado their home since their ancestors crossed the Bering Land Bridge. Mountain lions also have always lived here and play an important role in our ecosystem.

When living or visiting this area, remember that you are sharing it, and as animals at the top of the chain, you are responsible for changing your habits to coexist with these other creatures. What that means, is being informed, first of all.

Anyone living in the metro area heard about the Conifer bear story. Terrified residents there thought a bear was trying to break into their house, so they called their neighbors, who quickly came over and took care of the situation. When they were finished, the bear and her two cubs were shot down from a tree dead. The bears allegedly were not causing any harm, just sniffing around the house, yet they scared the residents enough that the residents took drastic measures.

Other species have also fared badly. Mountain goats along the road to the top of Mt. Evans have been fed so much food from tourists that their teeth are rotting, their birth rates are down, and they are becoming dependent on humans for their food. In a recent summer, goats butted tourists in their demand for food, and a baby goat was killed on the highway where she was scavenging.

Since 1980 there has been a 66 percent increase in the elk population in the area. That increase corresponds with an influx of mountain lions and other predators who feed off these elk. Although this means that there are numerous opportunities to see these great creatures, conflicts between humans and animals occur. There is a plan underway by the Colorado Division of Wildlife to manage the growing elk population. However, doing your part will help with all wildlife concerns.

Bring all food in at night.
Bring your pets inside at night.
Hang bird seed, suet, and hummingbird feeders on a wire between trees instead of on a deck or porch. Bring in all bird feeders at night.
Install outdoor lighting.
Keep trash locked up or inside.
Learn about the different species of animals where you live-their hunting and gathering habits, their lifestyles.
Learn about weather conditions that may affect predators' habits (a drought, for example, that leaves bears scavenging for food).
Never feed any wild animals!
Remove any dead carcasses from your property.
Try to plant only native vegetation.

The Colorado Division of Wildlife publishes numerous brochures on how to live with wildlife, including an informative brochure, "Don't Tempt With Twinkies," which describes the risks of feeding wild animals.

Prevent these unwanted encounters by taking precautions and learning everything you can. Remember that part of the joy of living or visiting here is the chance to see these awesome creatures in their natural habitat. Keep them wild. To find out more or to report a non-life threatening encounter, call the **Colorado Division of Wildlife** (303-291-7227) Monday-Friday 7 a.m.-5 p.m.

WOODCUTTING

Another pleasure of living here is being able to have a toasty fire on a chilly night and to heat your house with a wood stove. Because of smog problems, Denver often has restrictions on wood burning, but up in the foothills, this is usually not the case. Besides buying wood from stores and dealers, you can go out and get your own, with a permit.

The simplest way to get wood is at the **Jefferson County Open Space Firewood Sale**. Beginning at the end of August, permits go on sale at their administrative office (700 Jefferson County Parkway, Suite 100, Golden; 303-271-5925) Permits are $25 for a regular pick-up load and $20 for a compact pickup. With a permit, you can then make an appointment to pick up the wood, already stacked in tree-length piles, at one of the open space parks appointed that year. Ponderosa Pine, Lodgepole Pine, and Douglas Fir are usually available in sizeable proportions. You'll need a chain saw to cut the wood and a vehicle to transport it.

Arapaho and Pike National Forests offer other wood retrieval options. You buy a permit for $20/cord and then go gather the wood in one of the forest areas assigned that year. There is usually both standing and downed wood available, and it takes a bit more work. You'll need a chainsaw and vehicle and some good strong help. Permits are sold starting in May and June, and the earlier you get out there the better. Call the **Clear Creek Ranger District** (303-567-2901) or the **South Platte Ranger District** (303-275-5610) for more information.

Chapter Nine
Sample Itineraries

If you don't feel like planning, but want to enjoy a day in the mountains, try one of the following itineraries. Time of year, approximate cost, and the preparation needed are listed as well as the page numbers where you can find additional details in this guide.

A DAY WITH THE KIDS — SUMMER

When the kids need to get out, or you just want to go be a kid yourself, try this plan.

In the morning,
Head to the oldest miniature town in the United States, Tiny Town, where you can explore the tiny houses, exact replicas of many historical buildings, and ride on a genuine miniature steam-powered railroad. Kids get to see things at their level, and they'll love it (pg. 44).

For lunch,
Coney Island makes a good lunch spot and is just up the road on Highway 285. Hamburgers, hot dogs, fries, and thick shakes are the rule here and much better than McDonald's. The shape of the building, a hot dog with all the fixin's, should keep the kids amused (pg. 94).

After lunch,
Come down from the foothills in the afternoon and head to Big Soda Lake in Bear Creek Lake Park where the kids can go swimming and play on the sand beach (pg. 89).

Season: Summer
Approximate Cost: $6/child
Prep: Bathing suits, sand toys, towels, sunscreen, cooler of cold drinks

A DAY WITH THE KIDS — WINTER

Here's an itinerary similar to the preceding one but with a winter focus. When you're getting cabin fever and the kids are getting restless, it's time to get out.

In the morning,
Go sledding! There are several great hills in the area perfect for cold fun (pg. 87). Check out the Morrison Natural History Museum, a good hands-on museum, where kids can hold reptiles, dig out dinosaur bones, and stain a fossil cast (pg.33).

For lunch,
Go to McDonald's in Bergen Park, near the Walmart, where there's an inside playground, or eat at the Morrison Inn which serves Mexican food with a lively atmosphere (pg. 99).

After lunch,
Ice skating on Evergreen Lake is always a good time on a cold day. Kids can even rent hockey equipment and expend some energy playing a pickup hockey game (pg. 79).

Season: Winter
Approximate Cost: $10/child
Prep: Warm clothes, especially mittens and thick socks, your own ice skates and hockey sticks (if you have them. You can also rent), sleds, toboggans, or snow saucers, sunscreen

DREAMING OF WATER

When you find yourself parched from the Colorado sun and thinking of cool ocean breezes and water, try out this day of fun.

For breakfast,
Go to the Dream Café with a "Mermaid" or "Hawaiian" bagel panini sandwich, fresh juices, and homemade baked goods (pg. 96).

In the morning,
Then, if you're feeling adventurous, arrange for a water skiing lesson on Little Soda Lake in Bear Creek Lake Park (pg. 90). If not so adventurous, rent one of the paddle boats or canoes on Evergreen Lake. Relax, enjoy the mountain views (pg. 56).

For lunch,
Head up to Maxwell Falls for a picnic and to enjoy the spray of water. Dip your feet in, carefully, and cool off (pg. 73).

In the evening,
Either treat yourself to dinner at the Chart House where the oaken décor and fresh seafood specialities almost make you believe you're on the coast (pg. 93). Or, head to Bear Creek Tavern where you can grab a beer, have a good American meal, and watch the ducks and Bear Creek roll on by (pg. 35).
Season: Summer—May/June/early July
Approximate Cost: $30-52/person (the higher figure if you head to the Chart House)
Prep: Bathing suit, towels, shorts, T-shirt, sunglasses, sunscreen, water

FIND YOUR INNER PEACE

This day is sure to relax you for a minimal cost. Enjoy nature and quiet peaceful places.

In the morning,
Whether or not you are a Catholic, there is something spiritually inspiring about a trip to the Mother Cabrini Shrine. The shrine overlooks the rolling foothills and Denver below and seems quietly removed from it all. There's a statue of Jesus at the very top and stations of the cross along the way with benches and beautiful flower gardens for contemplation (pg.42).
For lunch
Go to the River Sage which is mystical and reverent along the banks of Bear Creek. The mission behind the restaurant is in part to pass on some of the wisdom of the Old River Sage, whose life reflected tranquility and gentle energy. Gain inspiration and feed your body some wholesome food at this Evergreen restaurant (pg. 101).
After lunch,
If it's spring or summertime, take some time to explore the Golden Watershed area where there are acres of pristine land and a few trails. The trail is only open to foot and horse travel, so it's usually quiet and peaceful (pg. 72). If it's winter, one of the novice cross-country ski trails is a good escape into the winter woods. South Chicago Creek and Idaho Springs Reservoir are both relatively easy trails (pg. 85). You can rent skis at one of the locations listed in the skiing subsection.
End of the day,
Finish your day by enjoying the geo-thermal caves at Indian Springs Resort in Idaho Springs. Over 100 years old, these caves are filled with mineral water of varying temperatures. Signs remind patrons to remain quiet (pg.37).
Season: Any time

Approximate Cost: $20/person
Prep: Comfortable walking shoes, water, towel, cross-country skis (if you have them, during the winter), sunscreen, a journal or good book

FULL OF ENERGY DAY

When you wake up and don't feel like doing housework or yardwork, and you've got the bug to explore and take advantage of the day, you might want to try this itinerary. Warning: you will be tired by the time you're finished, but what a fulfilling day!

In the morning,

Get out your mountain bike or rent one (pg. 47) and head to Elk Meadow Open Space Park where there are several trails to get you moving. The most challenging is the route up Bergen Peak and is sure to test your skills and stamina. The Meadow View Trail in the same part is quite a bit easier, a lot of fun, but also a workout (pg. 48 and 52).

For lunch,

Grab a bite to eat at the Wildflower Café. It's excellent food in a fun energetic atmosphere (pg. 105).

After lunch,

If you still have energy, drive up toward Mt. Evans and stop at the pullout for Chief Mountain Trail. It's a quick trip up, but a steady climb, and you're rewarded with an awesome 360-degree view at the top (pg. 69). Come back to Evergreen, take a walk around the lake or a jog, if you still feel inclined, and get ready for a night of dancing.

End of the day,

To top off the day, check out the varied nightlife scene at the Little Bear where you might find any music from rockabilly to blues. There are pool tables, a dance floor, and plenty of room to mingle. Check and see whether a national band is playing because you'll need tickets if that's the case (pg. 36).

Season: Late spring, early fall, summer
Approximate Cost: $25/person (more if you need to rent bikes)
Prep: Mountain bike (if you have one), comfortable shoes, water, energy snack food, sunscreen

NOT ENOUGH ENERGY DAY

You wake up, and it's a glorious day, but you just don't have the energy to go for a hike or bike ride (or maybe you did it all the day before in the "Full of Energy Day").

Afternoon,

The best thing you could do would be to drive up Mt. Evans and take along your camera. If it's not peak season, and the road's still open, take your time, bring a boxed lunch (maybe pick something up from J. Williams, (pg. 99). Take a lot of photos and enjoy. (pg. 22)

Dinner

Let someone else do the cooking at one of the area's many restaurants. El Rancho is a good choice. (pg. 97)

End of the day,

Finish off with a movie at the Bergen Cinema, which plays first-run movies at reasonable prices. (pg. 20)

Season: Summer-early fall

Approximate Cost: $7 and up, depending on which restaurant you choose

Prep: Camera, picnic lunch, book

PAMPER YOURSELF

Ok, it's going to cost some money, and you need to make a few of these arrangements ahead of time, but you deserve it. You'll feel as if you took a short vacation and will emerge happy and relaxed. Guaranteed.

During the day,

Try either the half-day or full-day escape at Tall Grass, one of this country's best day spas. You'll be pampered with a facial, massage, nail services, and spa lunch. Or choose just one of their services. The drive out there is breathtaking and relaxing in itself (pg.37). Take a hike at one of the Jefferson County Open Space Parks. Alderfer/Three Sisters and Meyer Ranch are close by and offer many quiet trails (pg. 73-74).

For dinner,

Treat yourself to The Bistro. The cuisine is fresh and a selection of hot and cold tapas are refreshing and all you need. On weekends, there is live music, and there's always a warm ambiance. Jefferson County has voted this its best restaurant. Enjoy! Reserve a table on the inside patio for a bit more privacy (pg. 92).

After dinner,

There's mountain theater. Whether it's Morrison, Conifer, or Evergreen, there's usually a classy, fun production going on. Call or check out the local papers for listings (pg.38).

Season: Any time

Approximate Cost: $80-300/person (the higher figure if you treat yourself to a full-day escape at Tall Grass and indulge at the Bistro)

Prep: Call to reserve at Tall Grass (a month in advance) and make theater reservations (call for schedules or check the local papers). Bring comfortable walking shoes and water.

A WALK THROUGH TIME

Begin before history, where you can see how the mountains were formed and where dinosaurs roamed the earth. Then enter into civilization and learn how the communities around us began.

During the day,

Start your day at the I-70 Geologic Cut, formed 140 to 95 million years ago. Interpretive signs lead the way (pg.41). Then head to nearby Dinosaur Ridge where you can follow the tracks and bones of dinosaurs that inhabited the area over 100 million years ago (pg.31).

For lunch,

Red Rocks Park is the next stopping place and a good place for a hike and picnic. Here, the giant rock uplifts merge with the more recent social history, and you can discover both through a short hike of the grounds and a tour of the Red Rocks Trading Post (pg. 43).

In the afternoon,

For more of a glance at how the communities began, take a walking tour of historic downtown Morrison. Find the brochures next to the Morrison general store or at one of the area's museums. Browse around the many antique stores in Morrison (pg.16).

End of the day,

Finish your day with a drive up Bear Creek Canyon (pg. 10-11), following the road the wagons used to travel to Evergreen.

Season: All year

Approximate Cost: Free

Prep: Walking shoes, water, sunscreen, picnic lunch.

Appendix

CELEBRATION CENTERS

0-50 GUESTS
The Dailey Cabin

50-100 GUESTS
El Rancho Village
Evergreen Memorial Park
  (inside)
Foss Park and Chapel

100-200 GUESTS
Boettcher Mansion
Brook Forest Inn
Chief Hosa Lodge
Crystal Rose/Robin's Nest
Evergreen Conference Center
Evergreen Lake House
Evergreen South
The Pines at Genesee
Willow Ridge

200 GUESTS AND UP
Evergreen Memorial Park
  (outside)
Evergreen Elks Lodge
Heritage Grove
Mount Vernon Country Club

LODGING

BY PRICE
Price Codes:
$—60-75
$$—75-100
$$$—100 and up

$
Evergreen Bed & Breakfast

$$
Ashley House Bed & Breakfast
Bauer's Spruce Island Chalets
Bear Creek Cabins
Crystal Lake Resort
The Horton House Bed &
  Breakfast
Mountain View Bed &
  Breakfast

$$$
The Abundant Way Chalet
Bears Inn Bed & Breakfast
Brook Forest Inn
Cliff House Lodge
Evergreen Lodge
The Highland Haven
Meadow Creek Bed &
  Breakfast
White Buffalo Lodge

LODGING

RESTAURANTS

BY LOCATION

BY CUISINE

EVERGREEN
The Abundant Way Chalet
Bauer's Spruce Island Chalets
Bear Creek Cabins
Bears Inn Bed & Breakfast
Brook Forest Inn
Evergreen Lodge
The Highland Haven

I-70 CORRIDOR
Ashley House Bed & Breakfast
Evergreen Bed & Breakfast

INDIAN HILLS
Mountain View Bed &
  Breakfast

MORRISON
Cliff House Lodge
The Horton House Bed &
  Breakfast

PINE
Crystal Lake Resort
Meadow Creek Bed &
  Breakfast
White Buffalo Lodge

AMERICAN
The Bistro
Buck Snort Saloon
Coney Island
Dream Café
El Rancho Village
The Fort
J. William's Café
River Sage
The Roundup Grill
Wildflower Café

ASIAN
Coal Mine Dragon
Thuy Hoa of Evergreen

BARBECUE
Dick's Hickory Dock
Hog Heaven
Rib Crib

CONTINENTAL
Tivoli Deer

ITALIAN
Italian Touch
Tony Rigatoni's Pizza and Pasta

MEXICAN
Morrison Inn
Whippletree

STEAK AND SEAFOOD
Chart House

RESTAURANTS

OPEN SPACE PARKS

BY PRICE

Price Codes (per plate):
$—Under 10
$$—10-20
$$$—20-30
$$$$—30 and up

$

Buck Snort Saloon
Coal Mine Dragon
Coney Island
Hog Heaven
Italian Touch
Morrison Inn
Whippletree
Wildflower Cafe

$$

Dick's Hickory Dock
Dream Café
El Rancho Village
J. Williams Café
Rib Crib
River Sage
The Roundup Grill
Thuy Hoa
Tony Rigatoni's Pizza and Pasta

$$$

The Bistro
Chart House

$$$$

The Fort
Tivoli Deer

All of the open space parks in the Greater Evergreen area are listed here. Some of these have not been listed elsewhere in the guide but do offer many recreational opportunities.

ALDERFER/THREE SISTERS

Location: Evergreen
Access: Take I-70 to Evergreen. Follow Evergreen Parkway into Evergreen. Turn south on Highway 73 and go to Buffalo Park Road (at the Evergreen Public Library). Go west one mile to the east parking lot. Continue 1/2 mile to the west parking area.
Size: 770 acres
Features: Gigantic rock outcroppings—"The Three Sisters" and "The Brother." Wildflowers, many birds, and small wildlife.
Activities: Cross-country skiing, hiking, jogging, mountain biking, picnicking, snowshoeing.
Trails listed in this guide: Biking—Evergreen Mountain Loop Trail; Hiking—The Three Sisters and The Brother Trails

APEX

Location: Golden
Access: Take I-70 to the Morrison exit. Head north toward Golden

and turn into Heritage Square. Use the northeast corner parking lot (lower parking lot).
Size: 530 acres
Features: Historical ruins. Urban vistas and secluded trails.
Activities: Hiking, horseback riding, mountain biking.
Trails listed in this guide: None

DEER CREEK CANYON

Location: Deer Creek Canyon
Access: Take Highway 285 south to South Turkey Creek Road (near Indian Hills). Turn south and go until you reach Deer Creek Canyon Road. Follow this past Phillipsburg until you reach Grizzly Drive and Deer Creek Canyon Park.
Size: 1,721 acres
Features: Diverse environments. Wildlife.
Activities: Cross-country skiing, hiking, horseback riding, jogging, mountain biking, snowshoeing.
Trails listed in this guide: None

ELK MEADOW

Location: Evergreen
Access: From Denver, take I-70 west to the Evergreen exit. Follow Evergreen Parkway to Lewis Ridge Road and turn right; parking is right there. Or take Evergreen Parkway to Stage Coach Boulevard. Turn right and go 1.25 miles where there is a parking lot.
Size: 1,280 acres

Features: Diverse ecosystems and wildlife. Mount Evans elk herd—fall through late spring. Two wildlife preserves within the park.
Activities: Cross-country skiing, hiking, jogging, horseback riding, mountain biking, snowshoeing, wildlife viewing.
Trails listed in this guide: Biking—Bergen Peak Trail, Meadow View Trail.

THE HOGBACK

Location: Morrison
Access: Take I-70 from Denver to the Morrison exit. Turn south and parking lot is on your right or the west side of the road.
Size: 630 acres
Features: Unique geological features, long trail.
Activities: Hiking, jogging, mountain biking.
Trails listed in this guide: Biking—Dakota Ridge

LAIR O' THE BEAR

Location: Kittredge
Access: From Denver, take C-470 to the Morrison exit. Follow Highway 74 through Morrison into the canyon. Lair O' the Bear will be on the south side of the road. The park is halfway between Kittredge and Idledale.
Features: Stream. Birds and beaver colonies. Wildlife including elk and deer. Handicapped fishing decks.

Activities: Fishing, handicapped fishing, hiking, jogging, mountain biking, picnicking.
Trails listed in this guide: None

MATTHEWS/WINTERS

Location: Morrison
Access: Take I-70 from Denver to the Morrison exit. Go south 1/8 mile and park is on the west side of the road.
Size: 1,095 acres
Features: Historic town site and cemetery, open trails, Red Rocks Park, urban views.
Activities: Hiking, history touring, kite-flying, jogging, mountain biking, picnicking.
Trails listed in this guide: Biking—Dakota Ridge

MEYER RANCH

Location: Conifer
Access: Take Highway 285 to Aspen Park. Meyer Ranch Park is on the south or left side of the road coming from Denver.
Size: 397 acres
Features: Meadows, wildflowers, wildlife including deer and elk.
Activities: Cross-country skiing, hiking, jogging, mountain biking, picnicking, sledding, snowshoeing.
Trails listed in this guide: Hiking—all trails

MOUNT FALCON

Location: Indian Hills and Morrison
Access: Follow Highway 285 to the Indian Hills exit. Follow Parmalee Gulch Road for 2.5 miles to Picutis Road. Follow the signs to Mount Falcon. Or, take Highway 285 to the Morrison exit. Follow Colorado Highway 8 toward Morrison. Turn west on Forest Avenue and north on Vine Avenue.
Size: 1,415 acres
Features: Sweeping vistas. Historical ruins. Lookouts. Picnic areas.
Activities: Cross-country skiing, hiking, history touring, jogging, horseback riding, mountain biking, picnicking, sledding, snowshoeing.
Trails Listed in this guide: Biking—Castle-Parmalee Trail; Hiking—Devil's Elbow Trail

PINE VALLEY RANCH

Location: Pine
Access: Take Highway 285 south to Colorado Road 126 at Pine Junction. Turn south or left and go approximately six miles. Turn right at Crystal Lake and follow the signs to the park.
Size: 820 acres
Features: Lake and river. Many birds and wildlife. Observatory. Handicapped accessible.
Activities: Fishing, handicapped fishing, hiking, star gazing.
Trails listed in this guide: None

REYNOLDS PARK

Location: Conifer
Access: Take Highway 285 south past Conifer to Foxton Road. Turn south and go 5.5 miles to the park.
Size: 1,260 acres
Features: Interpretive trail. Wildlife including wild turkey, black bear, deer, elk and grouse. Overnight camping. Stunning views.
Activities: Camping, hiking, horseback riding, mountain biking, snowshoeing, wildlife viewing.
Trails listed in this guide: Hiking—Eagle's View Trail

Bibliography

ALTITUDE SICKNESS
Bezruchka, Stephen, M.D. *Altitude Illness: Prevention & Treatment: How to Stay Healthy at Altitude: From Resort Skiing to Himalayan Climbing.* Seattle: Mountaineers Books, 1994.
Hackett, Peter H. *Mountain Sickness: Prevention, Recognition, and Treatment.* Golden: American Alpine Club, 1980.

AVALANCHE AWARENESS
Armstrong, Betsy R., Knox Williams, and Richard L. Armstrong. *The Avalanche Book.* Golden: Fulcrum Publishing, 1992.
McClung, David, and Peter Schaerer. *The Avalanche Handbook.* Seattle: Mountaineers Books, 1993.
Moynier, John. *Avalanche Awareness: A Practical Guide to Safe Travel in Avalanche Terrain.* Evergreen: Chockstone Press, 1993.

BACKPACKING
Harmon, Will. *Wild Country Companion.* Helena: Falcon Press, 1994.

BIKING
Barnhart, Tom. *Front Range Single Tracks.* Littleton: Fat Tire Press, 1995.
D'Antonio, Bob. *Mountain Biking Denver & Boulder.* Helena: Falcon Publishing Company, 1997.
Nealy, William. *Mountain Bike!* Birmingham: Menasha Ridge

Press, 1992.

Ryter, Derek, and Jarral Ryter. *Mountain Biking Colorado's Front Range: Great Rides in and Around Fort Collins, Denver, Boulder, and Colorado Springs.* Boulder: Pruett Publishing, 1998.

CLIMBING

Green, Stewart M. *Rock Climbing Colorado.* Helena: Falcon Publishing, 1995.

Horan, Bob. *Colorado Front Range Bouldering; Southern Areas.* Evergreen: Chockstone Press, 1998.

Hubbel, Peter, Bob D'Antonio, and Mark Rolofson. *South Platte Rock Climbing and the Garden of the Gods.* Evergreen: Chockstone, 1988.

COLORADO ATLAS

Colorado Atlas and Gazetteer. Freeport: DeLorme Mapping Co, 1995.

HIKING

Jacobs, Randy. *The Colorado Trail: The Official Guidebook.* Englewood: Westcliffe Publishing, 1994.

Keilty, Maureen. *Best Hikes With Children in Colorado.* Seattle: Mountaineers Books, 1998.

Rich, Dave. *The Denver Hiking Guide.* Telluride: 3D Press, 1996.

Ringrose, Linda Wells, and Linda McComb Rathbun. *Foothills to Mount Evans.* Evergreen: The Wordsmiths, 1980.

Salcedo, Tracy. *12 Short Hikes (in the Denver Foothills Central).* Evergreen: Chockstone Press, 1995.

---. *12 Short Hikes (in the Denver Foothills North).* Evergreen: Chockstone Press, 1995.

---. *12 Short Hikes (in the Denver Foothills South).* Evergreen: Chockstone Press, 1995.

HISTORY

Brush, Helen N., and Catherine P. Dittman. *Indian Hills.* Evergreen: Jefferson County Historical Society, 1976.

Chronic, Halka. *Roadside Geology of Colorado.* Missoula: Mountain Press, 1980.

Crain, Mary Helen. *Evergreen, Colorado.* Boulder: Pruett Publishing, 1969.

Fahnestock, Connie. *From Camp Neosho to the Hiwan Homestead.* Englewood: Quality Press, 1985.

Jefferson County Historical Commission. *From Scratch: a History of Jefferson County Colorado.* Golden: Astor House, 1985.

Bentley, Margaret V. *Upper Side of the Pie Crust: an Early History of Southwestern Jefferson County: Conifer, Pine, Buffalo Creek, Colorado.* Englewood: Bentley, 1985.

Sternberg, Gene and Barbara. *evergreen our mountain community.* Evergreen: Sternberg and Sternberg, 1987.

MOUNTAINEERING

Graydon, Don, and Kurt Hanson (editors). *Mountaineering: The Freedom of the Hills.* Seattle: Mountaineers Books, 1997.

NATURE

Foutz, Dell R. *Geology of Colorado Illustrated.* Grand Junction: Your Geologists, 1994.

Guennel, G.K. *Guide to Colorado Wildflowers.* Englewood: Westcliffe, 1995.

Wingate, Janet L. *Rocky Mountain Flower Finder.* Rochester: Nature Study Guild, 1990.

Watts, Tom. *Rocky Mountain Tree Finder.* Rochester: Nature Study Guild, 1972.

SKIING

Litz, Brian and Kurt Lankford. *Skiing Colorado's Backcountry.* Golden: Fulcrum, 1989.

WILDERNESS FIRST AID

Carline, Jan D., PhD, Martha J., Lentz, RN, and Steven C. MacDonald. *Mountaineering First Aid: A Guide to Accident Response and First Aid Care.* Seattle: Mountaineers Books, 1996.

Schimelpfenig, Tod and Linda Lindsey. *NOLS Wilderness First Aid.* Lander: National Outdoor Leadership School, 1992.

Index

About the Author

D. Blum

Kristen Blum lived in the Greater Evergreen area for five years and worked as a high school English teacher and freelance writer. She has written for national and local publications, served as news editor at DePauw University in Indiana, and worked as a reporter for several daily newspapers. She holds a B.A. in English and French from DePauw University and a M.F.A. in Creative Writing from George Mason University. Currently she is both a student and college writing instructor. She loves to travel, hike, camp, dance, and kayak. This is her first book.

ORDER FORM

This book is available in bookstores and retail outlets near you. To order your personal copy, simply complete the form below and mail it to the address below. Or you may e-mail or phone 1-888-879-9652.

____**YES**, I'd like _____ copies of *The Greater Evergreen Area Guide.*

Name _____

Phone_____

Address _____

City/State/Zip_____

Colorado residents only — please include state sales tax as shown below. Allow 30 days for delivery.

# of books x $14.95	_____
Postage and handling	**$3.00**
Colorado Sales Tax (CO Residents Only)**$1.05/per book**	_____
Total	_____

BULK ORDERS INVITED

For bulk quantity discounts or special handling please write, e-mail, or call.

Address all correspondance and make checks payable to:
WANDERLUST PUBLISHING
P.O. Box 31515
Seattle, WA 98103-1515
1-888-879-9652
email: wanderlust@seanet.com